John Furneaux Jordan

Character as Seen in Body and Parentage

With a chapter on education, career, morals, and progress

John Furneaux Jordan

Character as Seen in Body and Parentage
With a chapter on education, career, morals, and progress

ISBN/EAN: 9783337218416

Printed in Europe, USA, Canada, Australia, Japan

Cover: Foto ©Thomas Meinert / pixelio.de

More available books at **www.hansebooks.com**

CHARACTER

AS SEEN IN

BODY AND PARENTAGE;

WITH A CHAPTER ON

EDUCATION, CAREER, MORALS,

AND

PROGRESS.

NEW EDITION.

BY

FURNEAUX JORDAN, F.R.C.S.

LONDON:
KEGAN PAUL, TRENCH, TRÜBNER & CO.
1890.

PREFACE.

THE following pages have been re-arranged and for the most part re-written. The title too has been altered, and everywhere technical language has been avoided. The views and principles remain unchanged and unequivocal evidence of their truth is constantly brought before me. Few will deny that there are two clearly defined temperaments—the active or tending to be active, and the reflective or tending to be reflective. It is contended in this little work that the leading and remarkable feature of the active temperament is the absence of deep passion, and that the presence of passion is the leading feature of the reflective temperament. Character is never a chance collection of miscellaneous fragments. A given cluster of elements group themselves together in the more or less passionless temperament; another set run together in the more or less impassioned. The active and unimpassioned are quick, ready, visible, practical, helpful even when censorious; they tend to be changeable, they court approval for themselves, but are sparing in their approval of others, not infrequently they are self-confident or it may even be highly self-important. In the reflective and impassioned temperament on the other hand we meet with tranquillity (broken perhaps by occasional storms), repose, or even dreaminess, tenacity of purpose, and possibly a proneness to seclusion. Now and then, alas, we meet with indolence, self-indulgence, or morbid brooding, or implacability. It is contended further that each temperament has its distinctive bodily signs, which also run in company. The more marked the temperament the more marked and easily read are the signs. These conclusions touch a great range of character in every individual, but they make no claim to be a system: they have only an indirect bearing on many phases of human nature. Fine characters, and less fine are found in both temperaments. In both we meet with high capacity or poor, with wisdom or folly, courage or cowardice, refinement or coarseness. There are numberless varieties of character—many divisions, conspicuous types, intervening gradations, equal or unequal developments, varying combinations. In domestic and social life, intermediate characters produce perhaps the most useful and the happiest results, but the progress of the world at large is mainly due to the combined efforts of the supremely impassioned and reflective, and the supremely active and unimpassioned temperaments. As I have said on another page, both are needed. If we had men of action only, we should march straight into chaos; if we had men of thought only, we should drift into night and sleep.

CONTENTS.

CHAPTER I.—ORIGIN AND NATURE OF THE INQUIRY.

	PAGE
Assaulted wives in hospital	1
Their configuration	1
Character similar in both sexes and all classes	3
Bodily clues to character	4
Two leading temperaments	5
Shakespere's shrew	7
Change in character	9

CHAPTER II.—THE CHARACTER OF THE ACTIVE UNIMPASSIONED WOMAN.

Personal, intellectual and moral aspects	11
Influenced by capacity	11
Her habits, occupations, tastes, and judgments	12
Orthodox and conservative as a rule	16
In domestic life	18
In social life	21

CHAPTER III.—CHARACTER OF REFLECTIVE AND IMPASSIONED WOMAN.

A less striking personage	23
Not merely the reverse of passionless woman	23
Matures more slowly	24
The passionate and passionless as stepmothers	25
In the domestic circle	27
Sympathetic and approving	29
Temperaments in children	30

Chapter IV.—Character of Active Unimpassioned Man.

	PAGE
Similarity of passionless males and females	32
Disapproves of others: approves of self	33
Sense of martyrdom in passionless men and women	34
Is practical, active, popular	35
His morality	36
Seeks notoriety: extreme examples	38
His recreations	42

Chapter V.—Character of Reflective Impassioned Man.

Like reflective and impassioned woman	44
In character, sex a detail	44
Not mere reverse of passionless man	45
Is never a scold	46
The golden age and temperament	47
Summary of types of character	50

Chapter VI.—Bodily Characteristics of the Passionless and Passionate Temperaments.

Anatomical structures run in groups	53
Skin, hair, and bones open to observation	53
Different nervous systems have different bodily signs	53
Skeleton and figure and character	57
Ailments and skeleton and figure	61
Hair-growth in women, skeleton in men	64
Brief summary	66

CHAPTER VII.—BODILY PROCLIVITIES IN THE ACTIVE AND REFLECTIVE TEMPERAMENT.

	PAGE
Configuration of active temperament not due to debility	68
Active temperament. Less deep feeling	69
Marriage and family	70
Choice in marriage	70

CHAPTER VIII.—NOTE ON THE TEMPERAMENTS IN LITERATURE AND HISTORY.

Examples frequent	73
Brawling women and brawling men	74
Socrates and his wife	74
Godiva	75
Emotions earlier in development than intellect	76
Arthurs and Galahads	76
Lancelots and Guineveres	77
Nathaniel Hawthorne and George Eliot	77
Charles Dickens. Thomas Carlyle	80
Shakspere, Burns, Byron, and their wives	81
Temperament in the picture gallery	82

CHAPTER IX.—BODY AND PARENTAGE IN EDUCATION, MORALS, AND PROGRESS.

Nerve and the outer world	83
Nerve and science and art	84
Nerve and character, race, class, party, religion	85
Physiological errors of great writers	87
Education and body and parentage	88
Choice of vocation	91

	PAGE
More Sundays. Overwork	92
Progress. Body and parentage. Marriage	93
Shakspere	94
Test of progress	97
Art, science, and progress	98
Moral science and art	100
Vivisection	101
Bases of Morality	103
Chastity	106
Supernaturalism blocks progress	108
Non-supernaturalism	110
Poetry of future	110

ORIGIN AND NATURE OF THE INQUIRY.

CHAPTER I.

The student of character and human nature may gain much and varied information in the hospital ward. The opportunity of gaining this information was, at one time, freely open to me. The views I was then led to form have been fully and independently tested by competent and unbiassed observers in the larger world of health and activity. Several years ago I noticed that the women who came into our hospitals suffering from injuries inflicted by their husbands, had as a rule something peculiar in their personal appearance. The peculiarity or peculiarities seemed common to all of them. They differed in some mysterious way from the women who were admitted for purely accidental injuries. They certainly had not been assaulted because they were old or plain. It is one of the dangers of unbelief, so we are frequently told, that unbelievers will put aside wives who have lost their youth and youthful looks. Many of these women were young; some were very pretty; their husbands were all believers.

I came to see, slowly and by degrees, that the skin of the assaulted women was thin; it had, as a rule, little pigment, and was often brightly and delicately pink. Their hair-growth was notably spare; their eyebrows were scanty or almost absent; the hair on their heads was short and thinly scattered. Many of them, though not all, tended to be stout. In their figures or skeletons also (the skeleton determines the figure) they were unlike their hospital companions. They seemed to stoop, some little, others much. Their backs were inclined to be round, being more or less convex from shoulder to shoulder, and from neck to waist. They carried their heads and shoulders a little forwards. In all these matters they were unlike the occupants of the neighbouring beds, many of whom had abundant eyebrows and copious hair-growth generally. Very curiously when the hair-growth was rich I found a different figure or skeleton; the spine was straight, the head easily and naturally upright, the shoulders poised backwards, and the back itself was flat or even slightly hollow or concave transversely between the shoulders. The skin too was more freely pigmented. The women with straight spines, flat backs, richer hair-growth, and darker skins, tended to be thin, but were not at all invariably so. In appearance a few were handsome, some were comely, not a small number were more or less plain.

The friends and neighbours often let it be known by nods and winks, helped out by a few words, that the ill-treated and injured creatures whom they had brought to hospital had "sharp tongues in their heads;" they were slow to let an irritating topic drop, and always had a supply of such topics at hand.

Mr. Ruskin, in a few paragraphs of remarkable interest, declares that bishops should watch rather than rule; that their place is at the mast-head—not at the helm. What, by the way, would Thomas Becket have said to this; he who exclaimed when advised to be calm, "I sit at the helm, and you would have me sleep." But then Becket was, by temperament, the most self-conscious, self-important, self-remembering man in English history. A bishop, Mr. Ruskin says, not only ought to know everybody in his diocese, he ought also to know why Bill and Nancy knock each other's teeth out. In strict truth bishops are not trained to understand Bill and Nancy, and for eighteen centuries they have done but little for them. Bill and Nancy are what they are chiefly from organisation and inheritance, and in some measure also, no doubt, from circumstance. When fully matured, however, a body guard of bishops could not keep them straight, especially Bill, who is usually, and on physiological grounds, the greater sinner. Bill and Nancy will do better when we come to see that the improvement of educational, social, and moral methods has more to do with physiologists than with bishops.

There is no single feature of character which is confined to the poor—not one which belongs exclusively to the well-to-do. The respectable tradeswoman who asks a magistrate to protect her against a violent husband, and the delicately-born lady who summons an erring husband into the Divorce Court, resemble in organisation, hereditary proclivity, and character, their humbler sisters who fill hospital beds with black eyes and broken bones. Those unfortunate women came frequently, but not invariably from squalid homes. Often weak husbands had been driven to drink and outrage by excess of method and cleanliness and by slight affection at home.

I came to see very clearly too that there is no feature, or combination of features, and character which is peculiar to one sex. The fidgetty young wife who involuntarily provokes a foolish husband, is often in body, mind, and character, the counterpart of her father. The quiet, easy-going man is often the repetition of his mother. The difference of sex is small and secondary when compared with the fundamental differences of character.

Much of organisation and parentage, much of character, may be learnt in law courts. The good, or apparently good, who make charges are there; and the bad, or apparently bad, against whom charges are made. Judges themselves never rise above their own organisation, their proclivities, and their time. When theologians are strong, judges burn witches; when kings are strong, they imprison Hampdens.

The foregoing statements are not made for the purpose of extenuating domestic cruelty, or excusing the domestic savage. But every truth, if it is a truth, explains other truths. Look at two men of average—certainly not strong—character and organisation. They may be much alike in many ways. Both are but moderately wise and self-restrained. One marries a certain combination of skin, and hair, and bone, and nerve; he is happy and content, and thinks that everybody else, if they were only as wise and virtuous as he, would also be happy and content. The other, marrying quite another sort of anatomical combination, finds life arid and burdensome, and gradually turns to violence and folly. The first does not know why he is happy and good; the second does not know why he is unhappy and bad. Both are to a certain degree the creatures of organisation and parentage. The first has no charity for the second; perhaps he sits in a judicial, or editorial, or other chair of authority, and proclaims his own virtue by denouncing the shame of his neighbour. A change of place on the marriage morning would have changed their lives and views.

Here then was a clue, not to every nook and corner, but still to a great range of character. I gave this clue to one or two competent observers of both sexes who, it may be stated here, entirely agree with the main conclusions set down in the following pages.

ORIGIN AND NATURE OF THE INQUIRY.

Material for observation was abundant and within the reach of every observer. It was found in the voluntary confessions of weary men and women; it was found everywhere—at the fire-side, in the social circle, in the street, the shop, the railway carriage, the boat, the church, the theatre; in the inner life of various institutions; in meetings, committees, councils, parliaments; it was found in newspapers, and serials, and books; in poetry, history, letters, biography, novels; in the conduct of public men and women; in the productions of gifted writers, in gifted writers themselves.

In speaking of the less pleasing examples of both impassioned and unimpassioned men and women truth may sometimes seem bitter and words hard. The words will be used with reluctance. There is no truth, however, gleanable by moral means which ought not to be gleaned—none which, if wisely used, may not be put to some adequately rewarding purpose.

In the matter of character men and women may be put into three classes. One class (frequently called in these pages, because of its leading characteristics, the active and unimpassioned class) includes those who tend to be more or less ready, or even, in some instances, restless, busy, and quick; who tend, in their extreme varieties, wittingly or unwittingly, to imitation, affectation, and love of notice; who may also be fitful, or uncertain in mood, manner, greeting, and conduct; and who, while self-conscious, self-asserting, and self-approving, are given, so far as others are concerned, to discontent, disparagement, and candid criticism or censorious comment. One, or more, of these peculiarities may be strongly developed, and others may be difficult to discern. Some are more manifest in men, others in women. Women, for example, indulge in franker criticism and admonition;

they have more also of imitation and affectation. Men on the other hand display greater self-importance and desire for notoriety. In men, too, the habit of detraction is stronger and more uniform. The candid criticism of women is usually confined to the domestic circle; men carry it into social and public life. The men and women of this class, in addition it may be to other high qualities have, not rarely, generous sympathies, emotions, and affections. These sympathies, emotions, affections are not usually deep, but when they are associated with high mental gifts and are helped out by strong reasoning powers, the resulting character is often altogether admirable. Sometimes the emotions and affections appear to be almost, if not entirely, absent; and if, at the same time, the mental gifts are but poor the resulting character is not pleasing. The men and women of quite another class (called here, from its leading characteristics, the more reflective and more impassioned class) are those who tend to repose, tranquillity, gentleness, and who, under a placid demeanour, possess deep—if sometimes sleeping—sympathies, affections, and passions. These passions are sometimes worthy, and sometimes marked by turbulence or indolence, or sensuality, or moroseness, or cruelty.

The more extreme varieties of these two phases of character may easily be recognised; but there is continuity in character, in organisation and physiological proclivities, as there is in most matters, and a sharp line cannot be drawn between them. Many men and women, in organisation and configuration and in character, do not incline very clearly in either direction; *or they exhibit other and different tendencies so strikingly* that, whatever their organisation may be, they may conveniently and justly be placed in an intermediate class. The intermediate, like the other classes, comprises many grades of character, from high to low.

The active, ready, and less emotional or unimpassioned men and women form probably a large third of the community; the intermediate class is also a large third; a small third only consists of the more impassioned individuals.

The classification of men and women into the active and more unimpassioned, the reflective and more impassioned, and the intermediate, does not claim to be, or come near, a general or exhaustive classification of character. It has no *direct* bearing on many even of its leading divisions. It says nothing, for example, of the division of men and women into good and bad, wise and foolish, brave and cowardly. Nevertheless, in all probability the whole range of character is modified by the presence of unimpassioned or impassioned proclivities.

The impassioned character, let it be clearly understood in passing, is something more than the mere opposite of the unimpassioned; it calls for observation and analysis from an independent point of view. When dictionaries come to be placed on a physiological basis much will be altered in them. With common but perhaps not inexplicable inaccuracy, they associate anger with scolding. But the woman of slighter passions, or even a veritable "scold," is not angry, she justly denies that she is angry; she scarcely knows what anger is. Men and women who are capable of deep anger are never scolds. Shakespere, with all his marvellous insight into character, made the mistake which our own lexicographers make, or, perhaps more correctly, the word shrew was once used more widely and vaguely than it now is by those who measure their words. The fundamental features of character are never changed; Shrews are never changed into non-shrews. Catherine was no shrew; she was precisely the reverse; she was a passionate and rebellious woman. One passion may be changed into another, or its object may be changed, or its motive. Passionate rebellion may be changed into passionate obedience.

Certain features of character require to be carefully noted and analysed, because they are not characteristic of any special variety of temperament. Irascibility for example is not necessarily a sign of the unimpassioned temperament; it is not peevishness or petulance. Irascibility or quick temper is the too ready response to some cause—the cause may be slight, or foolishly inadequate, but it is there. Irascibility is frequently a pathological rather than a physiological condition. Gouty material circulating in the nerve centres frequently shows itself in irrepressible temper; occasionally for years, or even for a life-time, no other sign of gout may be present; then skin, or joint, or, perhaps, fatally changed internal organ may explain everything.

Neither is impatience found in the less impassioned only; on the contrary, it is often associated with the deeper emotions, especially if untrained. An anxious temperament is not a passionless temperament. The more passionless individual is less given (and herein is some compensation) to anxiety, or care, or fear, or despondency, than the more passionate; having no deep feeling he, or she, has no heavy foreboding.

Volubility is not peculiar to the unimpassioned. Sustained, orderly, punctuated, volubility is rather a sign of the emotional temperament, especially when it is found in capable persons, and above all in capable women. Volubility in the average, and still more so in the less gifted unemotional individual is disconnected, unpunctuated, endlessly repeated, and occasionally incoherent. Criticism, cynicism, churlishness, sarcasm, are not confined either to the passionless or the passionate; but in their harsher forms they are seen for the most part—singular as it may seem, in the impassioned class of men and women. Reproof, disapprobation, and discontent are not matters of habit in the more passionate persons, but they may be acutely marked when their causes are sufficient.

A fundamental change in character is extremely rare, and is probably never sudden; but such change may possibly follow severe injuries, especially of the head. These are unsuspectedly common in early life— in the nursery, the playground, and the athletic field —often thwarting all hereditary calculation. Similar effects may follow diseases, especially those of the nervous system. Powerful impressions, fear, sudden misfortune, or even sudden good fortune, as with injuries and diseases, may alter the state of the brain, and therefore change character. It is so also in very rare instances with the long indulgence of various strong emotions. In severe degree or where brain is unduly sensitive, they may even cause insanity—a condition invariably dependent on brain change.

Now and then a very slow development of brain and character *looks* like radical change: deeply-seated good or deeply-seated evil principles may come to the surface. Deterioration, or at any rate change, of character may come very early from early degeneration of nervous organisation.

More frequent are the changes of character which attend on re-arrangement and re-adjustment of its minor elements. A timid person does not become brave, or a bustling person tranquil, or a fitful person settled and tenacious; but the less fundamental features may so change that a practically bad character may become good—say timidly good or courageously good, as ground work is timid or courageous; or a good character bad—fitfully or persistently bad for example. Fear of punishment, hope of reward, good example, or bad example act in this way. Probably the characters which change in this manner are never very strong, but they teach this lesson, that in *practical morals* the importance of training and surroundings, especially in early life is of simply incalculable importance.

THE CHARACTER OF THE ACTIVE AND UNIMPASSIONED WOMAN.

CHAPTER II.

BEFORE we look more closely into matters of organisation and parentage it will be well to examine, with some detail, the character of the men and women whom, for the sake of brevity it will be convenient to call "the active and less impassioned" on the one hand and the "reflective and more impassioned" on the other hand. Women will be studied first because their characters, though not less elevated and estimable, are more direct, spontaneous, and natural. We shall look first at their personal, intellectual, and moral aspects, and then follow them into domestic, social, and public life.

The nerve action of unimpassioned women (and men also) is marked by vivacity and readiness rather than by strength or persistence. The active and unimpassioned of both sexes, but particularly men, who possess unusual ability, (and these are not few) are often conspicuous figures. And it is of deep physiological interest to watch, here and there, high capacity which is also self-conscious, fitful, discontented, and disparaging; or which is, in men especially, strenuously bent on notoriety, and keenly alive to the methods and opportunities of securing it.

The life of the unimpassioned woman of average capacity, and of all below the average, is often wholly occupied with little things—and she never rests. Very frequently, but by no means always—much depends on her training, social position, and surroundings—her restlessness takes the form of ceaseless cleaning; the rearrangement of furniture; minute and oft-repeated directions to servants, who are frequently changed, the correction of children, with fastidious supervision of their dress and her own; the denunciation of tradespeople "in these days," and the repeated recital of her "trials," or in other words, the shortcomings of others which come to the same thing. Her daily wonder is how "things would go on" if she were not there to look after them. She is surprised that she is not constantly told how indispensable she is.

Cleaning in her house never ceases. She seems to say, "See how clean we are; and to prove it to you, the moment this house is thoroughly cleaned, it shall be cleaned over again." When of the extremest type she unconsciously interpolates a clause of her own in the scheme of creation. At a certain period the Creator said, "Let there be houses, and women, and dusters;" then men were made to enter those houses, and humbly submit themselves to the usages thereof. She believes, with Lord Beaconsfield, that "the unimportant is not very unimportant;" she is perplexed however when he goes on to say that "the important is not very important."

In large affairs she enjoys the calm which attends on deference to authority. If authority is dumb she is dumb also—inwardly and outwardly dumb. In small affairs, and in affairs which are neither large nor small, she usually jumps to conclusions. She is much more interested in the colour of her linen than in the problems of her time. She refuses—she does not say this either to herself or to others, nevertheless she doggedly refuses to think of evolution, or agnosticism, or cremation, or the abandonment of oaths, or the use of libraries, picture galleries and museums on Sundays.

Here and there, where somewhat higher, but still not necessarily high capacity is present, the active woman's restlessness may find some social, or religious, or political outlet. She may become a zealous committee-woman and, Jellabywise, permit the African baby to thrust aside husband, and children, and servants, and household. The black baby, it is true, concerns her, but in strict truth her own position on its white committee concerns her much more.

The restless are always discontented, and the discontented are restless. The restless woman's discontent is not deep, neither, it may be added, is her disparagement ever bitter, or her resentment violent. When adversity is real she seems to behave like a philosopher. Her discontent is with small matters, a discontent which is captious at home, but bright and sparkling and chastened in society.

It matters not what the unimpassioned woman has, she prefers something else. If her house is full of oil pictures she prefers water colours; if her carriage horses are grey she prefers bay; if flowers predominate in her garden she prefers trees; the suburb she lives in is not so suitable as some other. She is probably content with the religion, the moral *code* (not at all with the practical morals), and the politics in which she has been brought up. In short, in her own little world, within her own domain, whatever is is wrong; but in the larger world outside—in society, in churches and chapels, in courts and parliaments—whatever is is right. If dire circumstances unhinge her she may be trusted to travel in well-worn or approved directions.

The spirited, indefatigable, adjudging, directing, reproving lady may, or may not, be our ideal woman, but, if not, she frequently has high compensating qualities. As a child she is singularly precocious. While still in her teens she is smart, self-confident, self-asserting, business-like; she can travel, shop, bargain, confer, and advise. She is little less wise, and she may be singularly wise, at eighteen than she is at twenty-eight or forty-eight. The field of vision of the unimpassioned woman usually wants range and depth, but it is clear from the first. The cleverer women, and these are not rare, give apt response to educational measures. They are quick to apprehend and have good memories; they see by a sort of instinct what their teacher wants and excel in examinations. They often come by indisputable merit to fill distinguished and responsible positions.

The highest aim of the educated unimpassioned woman, her chief success, and one of her greatest compensations is this—she is never open to ridicule. She knows the leading events in each reign, and the authorship of standard works in literature. Not infrequently her tastes are refined; and indeed, notwithstanding her domestic peculiarities, her feelings are kindly; she distributes flowers; she visits a district; she reads to the sick; she is usually hospitable in her own house, and as a rule generous everywhere. If she is more or less conscious of all these virtues she is nevertheless entirely sincere in them.

The unresting woman of education often reads. Respectability does not demand reading, but neither does it forbid it. Deferring to authority in one half of life, and jumping to conclusions in the other half, leaves a woman (or at least a well-to-do woman) considerable leisure. She must, however, have persons and action in her books as well as in her life.

The less impassioned woman is above all things a devout worshipper of respectability. Respectability comes to her embodied in two questions :—What will her neighbours think? and What will her fellow church-goers say? But, alas, respectability does little to lessen our infirmities. The common-place and passionless woman (too often a mere scold) of poverty-stricken thought and blunt feeling is given to disparagement, to uncharitableness, to petty gossip. It is not the theological woman only, as a distinguished writer seems to believe, who crawls up the judgment throne "to divide it with her master." The woman who lacks deep feeling leaps into every judgment seat, great or small—the small by preference—the very small. In the larger seats she is the mere mouthpiece of her accustomed pulpit; in the smaller seats she is herself. When Mrs. Cornwall is leaving home in search of health she whispers "that is not the real reason "—" Mr. Cornwall knows better than that." Mrs. Devonshire is about to keep but one servant instead of three: "What can it mean?" If it be suggested that Mr. Devonshire can only afford one, she scouts the idea as irrelevant; the vital question is, "can one servant keep Mrs. Devonshire's house clean?" The captious and confident and unimpassioned, of both sexes, pass sentence on all who cross their path. The weary who cannot carry all the burdens they would heap upon them—they are selfish; the calm—they are idle; the ailing—they whine; the desponding—a shaking would do them good.

Active, fitful, "disapproving" temperaments are by no means all alike. Their personal, intellectual, and moral qualities vary and are variously combined. But in both sexes there is one unvarying essential characteristic—the absence of deep passion. Love is simply preference; hatred is merely dislike; jealousy is only injured pride. They have not the sustained enthusiasms, but neither have they the periods of listlessness and depression which belong to passionate natures.

The unimpassioned woman of slight capabilities is not at home in the rarer atmospheres. Poetry stirs no emotion in her, and science excites no wonder. The capacity for surprise is never great where the feelings are slight. The degree of her surprise is, curiously, the same whatever the cause may be. If the cook came before her without a cap she would be almost as much shocked as if, on going into the kitchen, she found the cook's corpse suspended from the ceiling.

Her beliefs or disbeliefs are complete rather than strong. She has no convictions, but she has no misgivings. She does not believe, she adopts; she does not disbelieve, she ignores. She never inquires and never doubts. If she is reminded of Mill's doctrine that no opinion is worthily held until everything that can be said against it has been heard and weighed, she replies that "it is very well to talk, but all that Mill said was not gospel."

She is, as a rule, not only orthodox and conservative, she is more orthodox, and more confident in her orthodoxy, than the bench of bishops; she is more conservative, and more confident in her conservatism, than the house of peers. I am speaking of the women who are orthodox and conservative from temperament, not of those who are so from reason and conviction. Cardinal Newman declared, shortly after his elevation, that christianity was in danger of dying out before the end of the century if no new revelation came from above: our unimpassioned lady sees no danger. Every bishop's charge is full of alarm at the spread of unbelief: she has no alarms. The peers predict the ruin of their country and tremble at the onrush of democracy: she never trembles.

If the bishops and clergy, every one of them, were to sign a declaration, saying they had come to see that there was no evidence in favour of supernatural interposition, and therefore they had resolved to resign their posts in a body, she might possibly admit they were competent judges on matters of theory, but she would refuse to understand the propriety of their practice. She would go to church as usual the following Sunday morning, and if she found the doors locked she would exclaim, "Why could they not let things alone; they were very well as they were." The undoubting, passionless woman would form an ideal listener to the distinguished preacher (perhaps the most distinguished of this century) who advised his congregation to believe that the world was flat because the Bible taught that it was flat, and *at the same time* to believe that it was round because science said it was round.

Unimpassioned women are, more than others, the victims of surroundings. Having no passions, good passions do not save them from being abandoned among the abandoned; and no bad passions hinder them from being very good among the good. By nature they are never violent, or cruel, or implacable; neither are they ever "enraptured," or "lost to self," or "inspired." Passionless women neither tempt nor are tempted; but in practical morals many of them are quite open to the demoralising influences of curiosity, the fondness of change, finery, money, self-interest, and the wish to please. Conventionality imposes on the unimpassioned woman the socially convenient, but morally inconvenient, habit of *half*-adopting or *half*-ignoring the propositions of the moment. Hence she is able to meet the exigencies of to-day by reconstructing those of yesterday. Respectability, also, often demands that certain gaps in truth shall be filled up with falsehood, and certain exuberant truths be untruthfully pared down. In fact, to her, the principle of respectability is so overwhelmingly true that every detail inconsistent with it must necessarily be false.

Even the clear, unequivocal and abiding sense of duty which characterises most unimpassioned women of the fairly well-to-do classes is, in great measure, a ceaseless, instinctive obedience to the claims of respectability. It is not a spontaneous, sustained, generous, and irresistible impulse; it is not a reasoned-out scheme; it is not due to the selection of any given school of morality; it is not even, as she herself imagines, the product of a belief in supernatural rewards and punishments.

Just as a microscopist stains a tissue with different dyes to bring into view its various constituent elements, so we shall learn much of character if we watch it unfold in the domestic, social, and public atmospheres. If we look at the unimpassioned woman at home, and then in society, we see two apparently different and incompatible characters. She often brings to married life bright counsels and wide serviceableness, but she marries mainly from ambition, or a love of change, or in obedience to well-recognised custom, or from a sincere wish to enter a greater sphere of usefulness. It is pleasant to manage a house, direct servants, to entertain friends, to take her husband's arm to church, and to encourage all the proprieties.

If husband or child dies the sun is not blotted out and nothing collapses. There may, however, be genuine regret, and the ceremonial of "bereavement" will be observed down to its minutest detail.

It is popularly believed that a mother's love is greater than a father's. A mother's love is a telling figure of speech; but it is more poetically telling than physiologically true. If the father is of an unimpassioned temperament and the mother is not, the mother's love is the greater. But if the mother is unimpassioned and the father is not, then the father's love is the greater. Herein is another illustration of the fact that sex plays a minor part in the classification of character; some men and some women are passionately attached to their children; some men and some women are not.

In the family of passionless parents and passionless children, where there is no high capacity and no refined taste, the spectacle is a sad one: in it there is no rest, no gentleness, no guidance, no love; the parents perpetually harass; the children perpetually rebel. Too often, indeed, the children drift blindly, wildly, into the world; society is amazed and exclaims "how carefully they were brought up." In the prevailing ignorance of organization and inheritance the children are supposed to have been led astray by the worst feelings, and to have passed beyond the control and outraged the affections of the best parents.

It is in the family, at any rate in the familiar circle, and here only as a rule, that the deeper nature of the less impassioned woman and poorly gifted woman becomes unmistakably manifest. In the domestic circle she unbends. Here she is herself so far as she has any self. For she is physiologically so imitative, often unconsciously imitative, that in many cases she cannot wholly cast off the tone, or accent, or manner of her latest models or even of her late associates. If she relinquishes one model she instinctively flies to another, and the observer of a life-time cannot always discriminate between what is native to her and what she has, knowingly or unknowingly, put on. Usually, she puts her imitative faculty to good use and selects the best models. If Mrs. Monmouth has a good accent, or Mrs. Montgomery laughs musically, or Mrs. Somerset dresses with taste, she will talk like Mrs. Monmouth, laugh like Mrs. Montgomery, and dress like Mrs. Somerset. She is only very dimly conscious of her imitations. In her own home pleasing imitations are not so sedulously kept up; often, however, the ceaseless flow of disapproving and disconnected comment is not unrelieved. Cloud and sunshine come and go, but it is difficult to say when the cloud will come and when the sunshine.

Although the active, unemotional woman has keen self-consciousness she has little or no self-analysis. If she were plainly accused of, say, habitual disapproval, she would be surprised and offended. She would deny the charge and declare that the person who made it was "extremely rude." If by unwise and persistent effort she was made to see that the family group was uncomfortable and irritated she would exclaim that "some people did not know what was good for them." She believes not only that she is good, but also that she has the rare merit and rare courage of directing others how they may become as she is. Good is her constant aim. Her very self-consciousness helps her to be good. She never forgets who she is, where she is, and what her duty is. Not only is she unweary in doing good but she has many ways of doing it. She has one way of doing good to her family and quite another way of doing good to society. The household must be managed, drilled, and made ready for social inspection. Society must be encouraged and propitiated. The great public, too, is kept in view; its upper section must be impressed and its lower section kept in order.

The active, restless woman exists in many degrees and varieties. She may possibly surpass her restful friend in certain high notes of character. But again, on the other hand, especially when the intellect is dwarfed, she may have merely the outward seeming and garb of a woman behind which there is no trace of womanhood. She may be a sour, shallow, sexless shrew—an impostor as a wife, and one whose marriage is a fraud. The fruits of the imposture and the fraud are none the less bitter because there is no consciousness of imposture and the fraud is unintentional.

If, now, we follow the busy, unimpassioned woman into the social circle everything is changed. The rose tree is one of stems and thorns in winter, and another of leaves and flowers in summer. Home is her winter; society is her summer. If the door but opens and a visitor is announced, the transformation is instant. The sentence of the moment is broken off in the middle; it began in a rebuke to husband or child; it ends in words of endearment—the last words may be overheard.

The less emotional woman is by no means an ascetic. The true ascetic (of either sex), whose asceticism is hidden, unpublished, unsuspected, is probably a deeply passionate nature; not so the ascetic whose hair shirt peeps out at the wrists, and who commands himself to be flogged by gossiping monks. The woman who is pictured here is fond of movement, recreation, change. It matters little whether the incidents of change concern her condition here or her condition hereafter. Her busy day may open with a missionary breakfast, and close with a comic opera; she is an adept in combining the bustle of two worlds. She delights, above all, to entertain her friends, and to be entertained by them. In society she finds not only her work and her happiness, but her rewards and consolations. If a son enlists, or a daughter elopes, or a husband takes flight, society tells her she has been a "faultless mother" and a "devoted wife." She believes in society, and society believes in her.

In conversation, society's pattern woman (the pattern woman is rarely clever) throws out little or no light. If unconventional men and women, taking life seriously, discuss some of its problems in earnest words, she thinks "they talk too much;" and society agrees with her.

Although the active, unimpassioned woman is what she is from organisation and parentage, it must not be supposed that she is beyond the reach of surrounding influences. Poverty, misfortune, an unquiet bringing up, a bustling husband and bustling children aggravate her special characteristics. Tranquil circumstance, comfort, kindly training, and especially restful companionship, tone them down.

THE CHARACTER OF THE MORE REFLECTIVE AND IMPASSIONED WOMAN.

CHAPTER III.

CURIOUSLY the more impassioned men and women are altogether less striking personages than the unimpassioned. Their emotions lie less near the surface; their manners are quieter; their characters are more deeply hidden —more difficult to read. It is not always easy to predict, or to interpret, their policy, or conduct, but they will be consistent in opinion, and, as a rule, quiet in action. There is less to be said of them here because much has already been said, either by way of description, or comparison, or contrast, or suggestion. Nevertheless it is well that impassioned persons should be studied from an independent point of view, and in pursuing this task we will again look at women first. In its intellectual, emotional, moral, religious, or political—in its domestic, social, or public phases, the impassioned character is not merely the reverse of the unimpassioned. It does not follow, for example, because one cleans and is clean, that the other is dirty or indifferent to dirt; or because one is industrious, practical, or, it may be, talkative, smart, and superficial, that the other is taciturn, or dull, or idle, or dreamy, or profound. Neither does it follow because one is respectable, conservative, and orthodox, that the other is vulgar, or democratic, or heterodox.

Unhappily it is not rare to find in an impassioned woman either bad temper, or impatience, or irritability.

Her sarcasm, too, and criticism, and volubility, and reproof, may easily pass the line of discretion. She may, moreover, be affected, or unnatural, or formal, or fond of ceremonial, or unduly given to social excitement. But whatever else she may, or may not be, she is not habitually fitful, or restless, or captious, or complaining. When fairly capable she often carries with her an atmosphere of repose. Without knowing it she consoles and heals. She is outwardly calm, but, deep in her nature; feeling, and passion, and response to passion, lie—sometimes asleep and sometimes not asleep.

The girl of deeply emotional temperament matures slowly. Slowly her reason clears, her emotions deepen, her judgment ripens—always presuming that she is placed amid refined surroundings. At eighteen she is open, simple, trustful, childlike. In insight, in keen-wittedness, in resoluteness she is another woman at twenty-eight. At thirty-eight every charm of character is heightened. It is difficult to say when her best days are over. In her old age the weary find refuge in her quiet and experienced grace.

The early life of impassioned children is as a rule easy and tranquil, but it is not always unchequered. In both boys and girls, but especially in boys, occasional storms of impatience, and turbulence, and insurrection arise, these foretell good rather than evil and should be met by much calmness and indifference.

Early but undeveloped impassioned life is often full of unsuspected wonder and meditation. It is apt too to be dreamy, unpractical, and sometimes to be injured by excess of reverie and castle-building. Girl and boy have been told that beyond the stars other stars follow each other without end; but often, when perhaps they ought to be asleep, they cannot help asking, what comes after the last star? They have been told that time had a beginning and they marvel painfully on what *was* before it began. Their field of vision is wide but it is hazy; the figures in it are shadowy and they move with indistinctness. In moments of high health however and exaltation, which are often never forgotten, the figures, ideals, imaginary creations, and what not, come more distinctly into focus, and move with greater precision.

Opinion will differ as to which temperament furnishes the finest characters—the unimpassioned or the impassioned : it is well so; but perhaps the worst characters are found among passionate women.

It is often wiser to give heed to the warnings which lie around us than to admire the good—however abundant the good may be. Let us contemplate one grave warning. Let us enter the domestic circle and look at the impassioned woman as a step-mother. The cruelest step-mothers are usually impassioned. It is a physiological incident of extreme interest. They are women who, in ordinary circumstances, make the most affectionate wives and mothers. But their emotions are strong, it may be disproportionately strong and the reason, whether weak or strong—it is not by any means always weak—is weaker and is held in subjection. She loves too much perhaps; certainly hates too much; and most certainly reflects too little. Made to love, she loves her husband; but because she loves him, and because there is constantly before her eyes the evidence of her husband's love for another, she—slowly or quickly—flings reason, and judgment, and duty, and compassion to the winds. What matters it that the other mother no longer lives? She does not stop to think; she feels only and she is lost. Jealously she broods and ever broods until, step by step, the once open, affectionate, warm, sympathetic woman becomes something worse—something much worse—than a wild beast. An innocent child, unwitting of offence, possibly not very well behaved, possibly not very tractable (the second wife's child would seem full of faults in the eyes of a third if the second could but think of this), a child, made for caresses, is left naked and hungry, is pinched and beaten, is burnt and scalded, is imprisoned in dark closets or driven into the outer cold. Sometimes by a savage impulse it is suddenly slain. Sometimes with greater cruelty it is killed inch by inch. It is the darkest hour of life to contemplate these things. Well may the doubter ask "where is the special and foreseeing providence which counted the hairs on this child's head? which noted the fall of a sparrow from the very roof underneath which there fell another little unhelped and uncomforted life."

The evil is a physiological evil, and should its remedy come at any time it will come from the ever merciful physiological hand.

It is quite otherwise with the unimpassioned stepmother. For once at least her more passionless nature, perhaps her more unbiassed thoughtfulness, and her habitual deference to respectability, stand her in good stead. She does her duty. She treats her own child and her step-child alike. She trains them with equal care; dresses them with equal propriety; greets and dismisses them with an equal kiss.

Happily in the great majority of impassioned women the emotions are not only deep but they are also on the side of justice and mercy. Their morality also is associated with deep feeling. It is a feeling which (both in women and men) may run in a seemingly careless groove; or it may take a profoundly-reasoned and independent course; possibly the course it takes will not always fit itself to social or conventional standards. Duty itself, in the impassioned woman, is often a sustained and lofty impulse—not an imitation, not a deference, not a bid for reward here or hereafter. It is in the domestic circle that the difference between the unimpassioned and impassioned woman is most clearly seen. The less impassioned, it has been said, puts on her leaves and blossoms in society and shows her bare stems and thorns at home: the more impassioned tends rather to reverse the proceeding; the wealth of her nature is reserved for her own hearth. Here, if anywhere, she unbends; here are her quiet triumphs; here unsought tribute is paid to her; here are her losses and her sorrows; here, also, alas, much depending on intellectual capacity, her faults and weaknesses are seen—perhaps slowness to forgive, or implacability, or anger, or jealousy, or even the still deeper degradation born of uncontrolled passions. In one partly domestic, partly social aspect of life she sometimes contrasts unfavourably with her unimpassioned sister. She is less apt to think of the comfort and welfare of the absent. Delighted with the moment its companions, its incidents, she is disposed to forget others and forget time. There may, in some instances, be a scintilla of truth in the conclusion that the unimpassioned woman disapproves of the present and the near and approves of the absent and remote, but the judgment would be harsh and not infrequently untrue. She is, in strict truth, guided by *thoughtfulness* rather than by *impulse*, while the impassioned woman is too often led by impulse rather than by thoughtfulness. It is interesting to note the different ways in which the less impassioned and the more impassioned women receive the tidings of grave domestic misfortunes. Sensible and experienced women of both temperaments are greatly distressed—the impassioned are naturally most deeply affected. The foolish and inexperienced of both temperaments differ widely. The foolish passionless woman's thoughts turn to what is becoming in dress and the comments of friends. The foolish passionate woman throws herself into the exaggerated but quite genuine attitudes of a tragedy queen: with uplifted hands and streaming eyes she appeals to heaven and asks if there is any hope.

How the impassioned woman acquits herself in social or in public life depends partly on her emotions but possibly even more on her capacity, her training, health, experience, and years. She may be witty, entertaining, instructive, brilliant; she may also be silent, or dogmatic, or self-willed, or neglectful, or dull.

At home or elsewhere she is, as a rule, not difficult to please. In both domestic and social life, she spontaneously appreciates, congratulates, praises. She can soothe the vanquished and encourage the unsuccessful. In her there is compassion for all weak things—two-footed or four. When at her best, to adapt the words of a distinguished writer, she rises to the high and stoops to the low; she is the sister and playmate of all nature. Like George Eliot she can judge the unjust leniently, sympathise with narrowness and tolerate intolerance.

She may have much or little self-analysis; probably she has little self-consciousness or self-assertion. She does not say to herself, "to-day I will be good, and useful, and entertaining." She does not of set purpose lay herself out to be esteemed. She is genial, sympathetic, and appreciative without knowing it—certainly without intending it. When finely endowed her imagination does not (it is one of the dangers of the impassioned temperament) lead the judgment captive and her judgment does not chill her imagination.

Very curious and significant to the physiologist are the judgments which men and women pass upon themselves. Distinctly correct self-judgment is a sure test of high intellect, whether with or without the deeper emotion. Carping temperaments often believe themselves to be sweet-tempered; the appreciative often fear they are impatient and harsh. Frequently gentle natures believe themselves to be rough, and rough natures believe themselves to be gentle.

In purely intellectual matters the unimpassioned and the impassioned woman differ little when both are highly gifted. It is when the capabilities are poor that slight emotions, or strong emotions, tell so strikingly in character. Women, and men also, of great mental vigour, are mostly interested in the same questions and problems. Not infrequently, however, a different bias is visible in the two intellectual lives. A famous man—famous in the domain of action—once said that if he had not been a philosopher in deeds he would have been a student of words. The unimpassioned woman takes, perhaps, more to both words and deeds rather than to thoughts. She traces, it may be, the rise and fall of Shakspere's words. The impassioned student, perhaps, more frequently strives to get at Shakspere's exact thought and feeling. Nay, the thought-student, heretic that she is, would like, for her private use, a copy of Shakspere as he would talk were he now alive. She would rather speak of the suffering than the "sufferance" of the poor beetle that we tread upon. She knows that words and men have—must have—pedigrees, but the thought interests her more than the word, and, moreover, the man more than his ancestors.

Peculiarities of characters are, on physiological grounds, less marked in the earlier than in the maturer years of life, but still they are visible from first to last. As girls mature more quickly than boys, let us look at a couple—one unimpassioned by inheritance, the other impassioned. One is occasionally fitful and capricious; delightfully amiable at one moment, she has "her little tempers" at another. When she is in the nursery tranquillity reigns for a time; then suddenly discord and storm arise; perhaps no one can say how or why. The other girl, gentle, even, composed, it may be a little backward, may be a little dull, may be a little overlooked, is always, without knowing it or intending it, throwing oil on the troubled waters. The bright little lady is the general favourite. She is at home everywhere. She helps everybody. She is magnificently generous; in some of her moods she will give her picture-book to one playmate, her miniature tea-service to another, and even her doll to a third. Her little quieter, but more impassioned, companion is much puzzled at all this. Underneath a calm exterior lie the germs of deep and unsuspected feelings. Her sense of ownership and affection, ever for her toys, is so strong and tenacious that she cannot easily fling them away. The unphysiological observer calls—sometimes truly and sometimes untruly—one girl generous and the other selfish. Probably the tenacious little woman is not selfish; but she gives for solid reasons only, and from deep preferences. The doll of many quiet dreamy hours she cannot give at all. So, in like manner, in after, ampler, riper years, if her child is taken away, she is the more stricken down with blinding grief.

Let us turn now and look at two boys—young, but strong and active and firm on their feet. Say we are travelling with them in railway carriage or boat. One never rests a single moment. No human power could keep him still. He runs blindly hither and thither; he turns, and twists, and wriggles; one moment he climbs, another moment he tumbles; he babbles, and shouts, and laughs, and cries in turns. Perhaps an unimpassioned mother, the parent he takes after, is with him. She too is unrestful; she scolds and threatens, and chides, and now and then she caresses. It is all in vain. They may be better or worse from circumstance, but both are obeying irresistible anatomical conformation and physiological proclivity. The other boy is quiet in body, intent in mind, steady in eye. He may be silent for the most part, or possibly he may have much uniform vivacity. He sees, and notes, and remembers. He moves and speaks with an object in view. Perhaps an impassioned but tranquil mother gives patient and kindly replies to his queries, and points out to him objects of interest on the way. Now and then she may need to give a word of firm reproof. Both mother and child have their failings, but they also, in fundamental matters, are the creatures of organisation and inheritance.

THE CHARACTER OF
THE ACTIVE UNIMPASSIONED MAN.

CHAPTER IV.

In body and proclivity, as well as in character, passionless men and women have much in common. But they are not quite alike. In anatomy and in character men are more varied and intricate and less easily deciphered. Masculine circumstance has always been manifold and complex; and the fittingly complex men survived; men have had more to feel, to think about, to contrive, to avert.

The characteristics of the passionless temperament are seen in man as frequently as in woman; but the complexity and multiplicity of his character have more or less concealed them. And herein, indeed, is a powerful argument for enlarging and enriching and, so to say, complicating the lives of women. Those who do not object to candid comment, or who, it may be, admire it, would probably prefer to have it in small fragments and spread over a large surface. Make a house-keeping drudge of a markedly candid woman, and her candour becomes painfully conspicuous. Make a philosopher of her (she will keep house all the better for it), and her candour may lend one more to a multitude of charms.

The markedly passionless man, like the woman, is fitful and uncertain in temper and behaviour. He is given, in equal or unequal degrees, to petulance, to disquietude, to fuss or effervesence, to discontent, detraction, censure. He disapproves of everything of his own time or his own place. If his bishop has written a notable book—the bishop's chaplain collected the material. If a statesman proposes beneficent legislation—the idea is taken from the Roman code. If a physician puts forward a new healing power—the Germans have long been familiar with it. Here is a new piece of mechanism—its like may be seen in the museum at Pompeii. If his neighbours and friends could only see things as they really are, they would always keep themselves in the background. If they could compare themselves with their fathers and mothers, or if they knew anything of their French or German compeers, they would hang their heads with shame. In the City of Destruction the men who called Christian a fool when he was alive and praised him when he was dead were probably active passionless men.

In all his moods the censorious man is well satisfied with himself. His judgment is often at fault and his projects often fail, but he never ceases to place unbounded confidence in both. Sydney Smith, speaking of a conspicuous statesman of his time, said he was ready at any time to command the Channel Fleet or amputate a limb. Much more may be said of the extremely active, self-confident, unemotional man: if he had sunk half a dozen fleets, he would be ready to take command of the seventh; if he had taken off six limbs and lost six lives, he would be quite ready to amputate a seventh limb. He has an incisive formula for everything that is put before him: either it is not true, or everybody knows it already.

In the world of the busy, passionless man there is not room for two Alexanders: in his sky there is not room for two suns. Seeing, however, that other

c

Alexanders will thrust themselves not only into existence but also into notice, and that other suns insist on shining, he (it is so in some degree with the woman also) has a curious sense of martyrdom. He is always the victim either of injustice or misfortune. If he does not monopolise appreciation he is not properly appreciated. He may be well treated but he ought to be treated better. He may fill a high position, but destiny, he believes, fitted him for a higher.

The unimpassioned man—so by organization and inheritance be it always remembered—matures early, but not quite so early as the woman. He is brisk, near at hand, ready in suggestion, and practical in performance. He is fond of administration and of affairs of any kind—he is often an admirable public servant. At the committee of his charity school he is as much interested in the disposal of its dripping as in the selection of its chaplain. In company he is often alert, to the point, witty, and apt at retort. Experience helps him and he insists on getting experience. If he is fairly gifted (and the gifted man, as a rule, is kept in view here because he throws the clearest light on his class) he resolutely, confidently, and constantly shows himself. He would rather be the *known* chairman of a committee of three than the *unknown* benefactor of a nation. When he is less gifted he is probably not less self-important. Is he busy? He believes himself to be energetic. Is he sly? He believes himself to be diplomatic. Is he loquacious? He believes himself to be eloquent.

In contrasting the male with the female it will be seen that physiological restlessness and fitfulness descend more deeply into his nature. They show themselves not only in his manner and speech but also in his opinion, policy, action, and sometimes even in his religion and politics. The woman disapproves of small matters mainly, the man disapproves of everything small and great. The acid comment of the woman becomes petulance, caprice, waywardness, or actual discourtesy in the man. Circumstance no doubt explains much: if their spheres were changed, and especially if they were both of the extremer sort, the man would become a domestic scold and the woman a social mountebank.

The man, like the woman, has much self-consciousness and but little self-analysis. Like the woman too he is never the victim of imperious feeling. Neither of them is ever "possessed." Neither of them is torn to pieces by ill-balanced or kept calm by well-balanced emotions.

The very mistakes of the slightly impassioned man arise from deficient feeling. His intellect sees an opportunity of striking a sensational blow; his feelings do not step in and say, "the blow is needless, or reckless, or painful to others, or dishonest." The woman is kept from grave errors by her instinctive and instant concession to social demands. She also would like to be talked about but she *must* be respectable; the man would like to be respectable but he *must* be talked about.

Even the abler man of action rarely puts forth new ideas, or opens new paths, or sheds new light; but he is quick to follow, to seize, to apply, to carry out. He is always ready with a little avalanche of detail. He does not create atmospheres but he condenses them into solid utilities. His merits are genuine and he gets his reward. Creators of atmospheres are often forgotten —perhaps sneered at as unpractical, while practical men reap harvests of applause.

The unimpassioned man, more than the woman, is

exposed to divers collateral religious and political forces, but like her, his natural tendency is to ancient and revered forms of belief and policy. Special circumstances may sometimes lead him to contemplate with admiration the audacity of his own heresy. Opportune openings too for personal ambition may take him a long way from his political bias, but sooner or later he will probably return to his physiological moorings. It is but just to say that in rare instances the unemotional intellect is so lofty and commanding that no disturbing influence can hinder the formation of broad and just views in all the provinces of life. While, on the other hand, let it be fully noted, that in emotional men and women the narrowest views and coarsest prejudices are only too common.

The unimpassioned male, like the female, is usually strictly moral; but sometimes a feeble impulse may be attended by still feebler restraints. *His* moral difficulties are greatly due to his unsleeping self-importance. The determination to produce immediate effect often leads to later trouble—trouble which the boldest strategy cannot always turn aside. To-day, for example, he will say that Lord Chancellor Bacon was remarkable in that he shook off every superstition of his time. To-morrow, when told that Bacon believed in witchcraft and sneered at the telescope, he will declare that he had been wholly misunderstood; that he had, in fact, cited Lord Bacon as a striking illustration of the inability of the most powerful minds to free themselves from the errors of their day. If, again, fastidious listeners fasten him down to his first statement, he will petulantly exclaim that Lord Bacon's opinions are not of the slightest importance.

Sometimes, too, the more extreme passionless man is unable to see the difference between what really *is* and what he thinks becomes him, becomes his position, becomes his family, and becomes the public or social occasion. He constantly believes that the public see him as he wishes them to see him, as he sees himself— a sleepless seeker of the public good.

The public-spirited man of affairs displays much pertinacity (the pertinacity is too visible to be called dexterity) in getting on to platforms and in keeping rivals off. If in public assembly adverse fates have given him nothing to do—nothing to propose, or second, or support, or amend, or oppose—he will rise and ask for some window to be closed to keep out a draught, or, which is more likely, that one be opened to let in more air; for, physiologically, he commonly needs much air as well as much notice.

Whether on or off the platform he is especially prone to do what he is not asked to do—what, perhaps, he is not best fitted to do. His plans, however, are cunningly devised: he puts others in his debt and cannot go unrewarded. The really able and fluent unimpassioned speaker is often of great use on the platform. He is probably quick to understand his time, or at least his party; he sees its wants, expresses its opinions, warns it of impending evil, organises its forces, deals smartly with its opponents. His speech has much solid weight and reason in it; it is well planned, clear, convincing; perhaps it is marked by pith and epigram. But there is no passion in his words; the multitude is not moved; he is not moved himself.

The men of slighter feeling, like the women, have much imitative faculty. They show it in their speech perhaps more than in their manners or dress. This faculty helps them if they select a good model and do not follow so closely as to rouse suspicion. The latter effort often fails them. Sometimes, indeed, we can say quite positively that the eloquent speaker has changed his model, or perhaps we learn that he "sits under" a new clergyman.

It is interesting to note another difference between passionless and impassioned speakers. When powerful or unexpected assault drives both of them to bay, the brisk and entertaining speaker often becomes flat and disappointing, while the ordinary, it may be the tamer one, is roused to unwonted clearness and flame.

Self-seeking, scheming, vicious men are to be found among the passionless and impassioned alike. But the love of notoriety for its own sake is especially characteristic of the markedly passionless man. He is never consumed for any cause; he puts himself first and his cause second. If some undertaking, no matter how beneficent it may be, is not led by him, or done at his suggestion, or by his methods, he prefers that it should not be done at all. He predicts its failure and its failure gratifies him. He will champion any cause if he is made much of; he will deride any—if he is slighted or overlooked.

He is full of projects and prophecies and bustle but, unfortunately for his reputation, he never knows when to rest. When approved projects and bustle are exhausted, foolish projects and bustle begin. Society must be pleased if possible; if it will not be pleased it must be astonished; if it will neither be pleased nor astonished it must be pestered and shocked. It is difficult to put a limit to the pranks of the more select and extreme performer. He meets us everywhere—in the pulpit and on the platform; in law, in medicine, in arts, in literature, in journalism, in politics, in warfare. He is given to do "big things," sometimes useful sometimes useless—swimming a channel, or crossing one in a balloon, or sailing an ocean in a cockle-boat, or riding across a continent, traversing a desert, or cutting through a jungle. The performers are not all alike, and the big things may be flavoured with one or several flavours—something of exploration, or of search, or negociation, something of philanthropy, something of fighting. Our heroes are very fitful yet very confident: to-day *this* is the proper step, to-morrow *that;* each step is to decide the fate of a continent and the dignity of England. The man of larger action and of slighter judgment finds his true arena in the clouds, or on the ocean, or in Asia, or in Africa. His courage is beyond question. As a rule he remains single, and wisely so. His genius fits him much more for life on the camel's back, or in a boat, or in a balloon than for life on the domestic hearth or in the study.

The journalistic performer has great advantages; not only can he perform his pranks but he can print them. He calls upon the nation to suspend its avocations, resolve itself into a committee, and consider his proposals. The nation in committee must act quickly for his proposals come in quick succession. He is by temperament a prophet of evil. One day huge fleets are upon us from the south: why discuss trade, or politics, or morals, or religion, when to-morrow we shall have to fight for our lives. Another day we are defenceless against invasion from the moon: only fittingly placed aerial stations can save us. The crazes grow; the third day brings the craziest: old women in great numbers are being systematically thrown into the Thames. Not a moment is to be lost. Consider what might happen to our own dear grandmothers! Does a cold-blooded generation ask for proof? An old woman's corpse is secretly bought from the "shady" porter of the nearest parochial "dead house;" it is secretly thrown into the Thames; it is fished up again with much publicity and many flourishes. Dignitaries of the church, after secret consultation, publicly testify to the zeal and good intentions of the fisher. Let scoffers beware! Have they not themselves toppled an old woman or two over the embankment on a dark night? Besides if they do not keep quiet the saviour of old women will name them. The unimpassioned are all saviours. The acknowledged saviour is probably not ill pleased with himself. We can of ourselves do nothing right—but we can believe in him, think of him, talk of him, dream of him, thank God for him, call him saint and hero, and above all, ask him to address us.

To the physiological biographer there are two kinds of notable human life. One is the life of a set of limbs directed to surprising movements by singular but sufficient brain; the other is the life of brain chiefly, with sufficient limb power to satisfy its needs. One is a life of conspicuous energy and striking deeds; the other is one of more or less unobtrusive thought, or observation, or research. One crosses deserts, swims seas, ascends into heavens, descends into hells; the seas and deserts are ready-made; the heavens and hells are manufactured at will and, for the most part, out of flimsy materials. The other stays at home and quietly strives to see what lies around him.

Mr. Ruskin believes that all men who seek high position are influenced by love of approbation. A man desires to enter parliament that he may write "M.P." after his name. A bishopric is sought by one who would be called "my lord." A throne is prized because its occupant is styled "your majesty." There is no doubt some truth—much truth in this view, but it is not wholly true. He had the unimpassioned man in view. Here and there a man of strong passion, and therefore of strong conviction, strives to enter parliament mainly to promote a cause. Here and there a a bishop loses his dignity in his devotedness. Here and there in history a king has cared more for his people than for titular paraphernalia or court puppet shows. There have been those who would rather teach a nation than rule over it; those who would rather give it an idea than take a crown from it. Martin Luther (rightly or wrongly matters not here, convictions are not necessarily just *because* they are passionate) thought more of the supremacy of the Bible and the evils of papal rule than he did of Martin Luther. William Shakspere valued the success of the Globe Theatre more than he valued William Shakspere. The writer of Hamlet never dreamt that Hamlet would be printed: surely a remarkable incident, but one not recorded in histories of England which nevertheless tell us how many pairs of stockings Queen Elizabeth wore. William Lloyd Garrison toiled night and day, *not* for the celebrity of William Lloyd Garrison, but for the downfall of slavery; and when it fell he gladly hid himself from public gaze. But these were all deeply passionate men. The intellect is careful of name and fame; it garners them like "golden grain," while passion "flings them to the winds like rain."

We have recently lost a great statesman who, more than any other, has created our present political atmosphere, but who, while passionately caring for justice and mercy, has cared little for his personality, little for parchments and for formulæ; and therefore it is difficult to find his name in histories (Mr. Green's is one of them) which profess to " come down to our own time." Atmospheres are too subtle for historians. They discern only actors and actions. Yet even Acts of Parliament do not come before their fitting atmospheres and do not live after them. Magna Charta itself did little for freedom. It was kicked aside a hundred times—kicked whenever it crossed the path of kings or courtiers. It was only when freedom became the pervading passion, the physiological impulse of a determined although a patient race that freedom was safe. The passion was roused by passionate natures who forgot themselves, and who are therefore, many of them, unknown to us. History takes care of those who take care of themselves. If the unimpassioned thrust themselves unduly into view in our own day, they have assuredly thrust themselves unduly into the pages of history. Men were in the past what they are now. He who would read dead brain must first read the living.

The very recreations of the active passionless man are uneasy. He is unhappy in repose and rests nowhere long. After a busy day he must have a pungent evening. He is found in the theatre, or concert, or circus, or church, or the bazaar, or dinner, or conversazione, or club, or all these, turn and turn about. But these yield him no real contentment. The woman delights in social stir, in the visit, the tea-table, the dinner, "a little music," the "at home." The man delights in official position, in committees, sub-committees, deputations, councils, boards, parliaments. He is business-like and punctual. If he misses a meeting a telegram announces a more ostentatious call.

The teachings of physiology are exceedingly practical: they touch all the width and length of life. Perhaps at some future time a council of physiologists will select selectors, rule rulers, and inspect inspectors. They will say of one statesman, "he thinks too much," of a another, "he does too much." They will take from this inspector's praise so much discount—so much from that inspector's blame.

The passionless are not alike: one man is restless mainly; another fitful; another censorious; another thirsts for notoriety. All are alike in this—they are wanting in deep feeling. The passionless temperament exists in every degree. In one man it may be slight, or marked by high qualities, or difficult to detect. In another it may be so extreme that he can only be called a busy-body, or a buffoon, or a compound of both. As a husband he is not rarely an impostor and his marriage a fraud.

THE CHARACTER OF THE MORE REFLECTIVE AND IMPASSIONED MAN.

CHAPTER V.

Much, either directly or indirectly, has already been said of the more impassioned man. He resembles the impassioned woman more closely than the passionless man resembles the passionless woman. Passionless men and women are full of aims and projects; but the man's aims and projects are not those of the woman, hence the seeming difference—more seeming than real—in their characters. Not only is the impassioned man a sort of masculine version of the impassioned woman, he is much more like her than he is like his passionless brother. Sex distinguishes human beings from each other less than nerve, less than temperament and character. In character, at any rate, sex is a detail which selfish men have striven to magnify into a principle.

The more or less passionate men, like their sisters in temperament, are less self-conscious and have fewer personal aspirations than the more or less passionless men and women. They tend, as a rule, to be restful, natural, spontaneous, contented. They sometimes, it is true, change for good or evil the circumstances around them, but they do this not so much from deliberate purpose as from some indwelling and spontaneous force.

Theologians seem to look upon man as a combination of the divine and the diabolical. The elements may be well or ill-mixed. Ordinary mingling produces ordinary men. If rough fragments of divinity are large, the compound is called an erratic genius; if big lumps of the devil predominate, he is regarded as a lawless miscreant. With less of theology, of a certain sort at least, and more of truth, we may be sure that much depends on the quantity and quality and combination of brain and nerve structures. Combination is not enough, there must be quantity also. Goethe somewhere points to the sad spectacle of "ignorance with spurs on." The spectacle is less melancholy than that of a feeble intellect spurred on, no matter in what direction, by powerful passions. Carlyle says that the first gift of all men is to "have intellect enough;" which few persons will now deny means brain enough. It is well that blood and judgment or passion and intellect should be well comingled. He must have a goodly share of both, above all of intellect, who is not to be a pipe for fortune's finger to play what stop she please.

The more impassioned man is not necessarily the reverse of the less impassioned. He may spend his evenings in pleasure from a genuine love of it; but his pleasures do not change every hour, and he is not driven to them by mere restlessness. If he takes part in public work he is probably invited to do so from some special fitness; or it may be that he has at heart some movement which he wishes to promote. When his work is done he willingly retires. He is able to see what others can do better than he; and he would rather that his cause should prosper in other hands than fail in his own. He has a hearty word of praise for his own fellow-workers, his own friends, and his own time. His praise, too, is not merely lip-praise, or official, or ceremonial, or from policy; it springs from genuine admiration. Probably he errs in estimating too generously the merits of those around him: one is on his way to a bishopric; another should grace the woolsack; a third will one day lead the House of Commons.

The impassioned man is never, and indeed cannot be, an habitual scold. There are however as many scolds among men as among women, only we give them finer names. We are but too ready to call a sharp-tongued woman a scold, while, with the same breath, we call the scolding man a "thinker," "seer," "prophet." Praise is usually flat, while clever scolding, with tongue or pen, is always interesting, stately, and impressive. Mark Antony (who was no scold however) would have declaimed from a much humbler pedestal if he had said that the good men do lives after them, while the evil is often buried with their bones. Herodotus, it seems, is held in less esteem than Thucydides. Herodotus was given to genial praise; Thucydides indulged in stern rebuke. It may be added here that temperament compelled Herodotus to approve and Thucydides to disapprove. In every field of human performance he comes to the front who throws strong vitriol with a strong hand; he is thrust aside in his turn, but only when a stronger hand throws stronger acid.

There is much, very much, around us and within us which deserves scolding; but there is much also that does not: hence the exalted genius who scolds everything, evil and good alike, occupies a singular position; the wisest man does not speak wiser words than he; the greatest fool does not utter greater folly.

No generation is without its army of scolds and nothing goes unscolded. But there are stock subjects on which every recruit tries his hand and every veteran displays his skill. "*Our* time has one pursuit only—moneygetting; one passion—love of money; one religion—the worship of money." "In *these* days workmanship is but another name for shoddy and shams." In politics *now-a-days* "the people are blind and the leaders gelatinous." "*Modern* education" is a blasphemous conflict between divine providence and the school board—providence, and the scold, seeking one future for the child, the school board seeking another.

It is of little use to argue with the scold. Anatomy and physiology make him what he is. He does not know that he is a scold. He does not stop to think of his long ancestral line. But the scolded may be consoled. The evil of the present day is great and the good is limited; the good however is greater and the evil less than in any day gone by.

This also we may truthfully say: if there ever was a time when men were indifferent to wealth; when all workers lived only to do honest work; when leaders had backbone and peoples eyesight; when providence and the schoolmaster foresaw, eye to eye, each human destiny and the training best suited to it;—if such a time ever existed, it was an epoch cf greater significance than the Reformation, or the French Revolution, or the discovery of America; yet the epoch has no date, and the documents recording it have been lost or destroyed. Is it possible that the happy time exists only in the brain of physiological scolds? If so, historians and constructors of philosophies of history would do well to study brain more and parchment less. For if the golden age is a brain product, physiology determines for each one of us whether it lies in the past or in the future.

The *bare* facts of history teach the physiologist

much—teach much more than the elaborate disquisition of the purely literary historian: and the barest facts of history teach that scolding depends more on the state of nerve which lies inside than on the extent of wickedness which lies outside the skull. One example, which tells of the past and the present, will suffice—say the love of riches. Modern kings, and popes (it would be so with patriarchs and apostles if we had any), and cardinals, and bishops, and nobles may complacently compare themselves with their forerunners; and their forerunners, too, were neither better nor worse than their neighbours and their times. At one time no petition to the chair of Peter could be heard unless it was tied to a cup of gold: permissions to commit crimes were sold in the very courts of religion: bishoprics were bought for unborn babies: during long ages families accepted money for a murdered father or a murdered son: at one time great nobles built castles to hide stolen goods as well as cowardly skins. Sins grow or dwindle in company; and if greed is less gross in our time, so also is every other vice.

The contemplation of scolds is not without profit. Their prince belongs to our own century—a prince who gives his royal sanction to no one who did not live a long way off, or a long time ago: Goethe will do for distance; Cromwell will do for time.

The gifted scold may fling out burning words but in his inmost soul there is no flame. Or, let us say, a scolding genius may stir the fire with imposing crackle and flash but he adds no fuel to it and takes from it no heat. For the scold is never a passionate man: he is as little like a passionate man as a gigantic squib is like a volcano; the gigantic squib gives out brilliant sparks as long as it lasts; the volcano quietly sleeps and only now and then pours out its red-hot lava.

The non-scold interests us less, but perhaps he helps us more. He initiates, constructs, creates, encourages, it may be in little things, it may be in large. He who discerns even a little good around us and shows how it arose, how it may be increased or used, is a true leader —leader whether small or great. He does not profess to lead; he scarcely knows that he leads. The scold, save at his best—save when his intellect is of the highest order—is but a poor leader: he rebukes with a trumpet, he leads with a penny whistle.

The true *artist* in scolding does not scold without ceasing; he knows the value of a back-ground of praise. He condemns one thing more effectively by approving another. When he discourses on books and reading with unequalled charm; when he praises women; when he skilfully demonstrates that Shakspere had no heroes—only heroines; when he has a kindly word for the servants' hall; and when, above all, he scolds us with much pains-taking, and in the choicest words, we do not defend ourselves, we propose no reforms, alas! we simply listen. We listen gladly even when he affirms that in the education, the morals, the religion, the politics, the trade, the sciences and the art of *modern* times we are, all of us, travelling along the worst roads we can find and at the maddest of paces. We listen with delight when he declares that our political economists are wandering in the dark even though one light at least is offered to them; or when he tells our women that if they were all good they would put an end to war—they *could* do it by wearing plain black for a week; they *would* do it if the shot happened to hit their own china shelves: or when he describes evolution as a doctrine which attributes the birth of a nightingale to the marriage of a bristled brush and a whistling wheel: or when he exclaims that the sun does not shine as it once shone, nor the rivers sparkle, and that modern winds so distort foliage that artists cannot draw it.

When unimpassioned men preach the degeneracy of our race in modern times, we may be comforted. The physiologist, at any rate, knows that a feeble time does not produce powerful scolds; and no scolds have, at any time, come up to ours.

It will be well at this point to summarise briefly the leading principles which have now been put forward, and which it is the object of these pages to enforce.

Quite partial methods of classifying character are of daily utility. Perhaps the most important classification is that which puts men and women into two divisions or two temperaments—the active or tending to be active, and the reflective or tending to be reflective. To many students of character this is in itself no new suggestion; but much more is contended for here. It is contended that the more active temperament is quick, ready, practical, helpful, conspicuous, and—a very notable circumstance — less impassioned; the more reflective temperament is quiet, less active, less practical, possibly dreamy, secluded, and—also a remarkable circumstance—more impassioned. In the active and more or less passionless temperament the intellect predominates, and takes an unusually large share in the fashioning of life. In the reflective and impassioned temperament the emotions play a stronger part.

The elements of character are not a chance and miscellaneous collection—they run together in somewhat uniform groups. The less impassioned individuals, for example, are not merely active, quick, practical— they tend also to be changeable, fond of approbation, though sparing in their approval of others; they are often self-confident and even self-important. When the mental endowment is high and the surroundings favourable, the active and less-impassioned temperament furnishes many of our finest characters—great statesmen and great leaders; sometimes, especially when the mental gifts are slight, the character is less pleasing: love of change may become mere fitfulness; activity may become bustle; sparing approval may turn to actual censoriousness; love of approbation may degenerate into a mania for notoriety. In the impassioned temperament, on the other hand, we find quite another group of elements—repose or even gentleness, quiet reflection, noiseless methods, tenacity of purpose. The emotions, good or evil, are deep and enduring. In this class also, especially when the intellect is powerful and the training refined, lofty characters are found. In this class, too, are found probably the worst and most degraded characters. In its lowest levels we meet too often with indolence, self-indulgence, morbid brooding, implacability, or even cruelty.

Perhaps the most important teaching of these pages is, that a given cluster of characteristics run uniformly together in the passionless temperament, and that another given cluster run as uniformly in the impassioned. Next in importance is the conclusion that each temperament has its cluster of special, distinctive, bodily signs. The more marked the temperament the more marked are the signs.

These conclusions touch a great range of character in every individual, but they make no pretension to be a system. They have only one indirect bearing on many phases of character. In both the unimpassioned and the impassioned temperaments there may be found, for example, either wisdom or folly, courage or cowardice, refinement or coarseness.

It must always be remembered, too, that besides the more marked types of character, whether bodily or mental, there are numberless intermediate gradations. When the temperaments, moreover, are distinctly marked, the ordinary concurrent elements may exist in very unequal degrees and be combined in very various ways. One or two qualities may perhaps absorb the sum total of nerve force. In the passionless man or woman extreme activity may repress the tendency to disapprove; immense self-importance may impede action. In the impassioned individual, inordinate love or hate may enfeeble thought; deep and persistent thought may dwarf the affections.

For the ordinary purposes of life, especially of domestic and social life, the intervening types of character (combining thought and action more equally, though probably each in less degree) produce, perhaps, the most useful and the happiest results. But the progress of the world at large is mainly due to the combined efforts of the more extreme types—the supremely reflective and impassioned, and the supremely active and unimpassioned. Both are needed. If we had men of action only we should march straight into chaos; if we had men of thought only we should drift into night and sleep.

BODILY CHARACTERISTICS OF UNIMPASSIONED AND IMPASSIONED TEMPERAMENTS.

CHAPTER VI.

BRAIN and nerve, as we have already seen, are the dominant structures in the human body. That these differ in different individuals no one will seriously deny. There can be little doubt also that the anatomical structures in any given body run together in sets. With one particular kind of nerve—the kind is recognised by its physiological action—there will be associated a particular kind of bone, of skin, of hair, and of other organs. At any rate a great step is taken if it can be shown that particular varieties of bone, skin, and hair are found in special groups; if these run in groups, other structures and organs will run with them. During life certain structures only, and these but partially, are open to observation, examination, inference, and classification. Of these the skin, hair, and bones, especially the collected bones or skeleton which together determine the framework or general figure of the body, are the most important. And here questions of moment at once suggest themselves. Can the proclivities of invisible nerve be inferred from the more visible anatomical structures? The physiological actions of the nervous system go to make up character: can these be in any degree gathered from the skin, and hair, and bones, and skeleton or figure? It is the object of these pages to show that something may be done by way of reply to these questions.

The skin gives less information of nerve and of character than the appendages which belong to it. Nevertheless the skin will in many ways repay careful observation. In the less impassioned woman, whom we shall first consider, because in conformation and proclivity, as well as in character, she presents clearer and simpler features than the male, the skin tends towards thinness. It may be because it is thin that the cutaneous appendages tend to be scanty and poor. It is well to note here that a thin bodily skin is no indication of the existence of what is popularly called a "thin skinned" temperament: it is probably the reverse. In many women and in not a few men of the unimpassioned class the skin tends to be not only thin, but to be also clear, transparent, and pigmentless. The thinness probably permits the capillary circulation to be more easily seen, especially in the face, which is pink, sometimes vividly pink, and beautiful. To a strikingly pink and clear complexion there are often added extremely pretty features; so that if we consider the face and prettiness and colour mainly, and look less at the figure, we shall find the most beautiful women in this class. The more impassioned woman has frequently a highly coloured face; but under the colour are traces of darker pigment. The skin of the less impassioned woman is not always pink or white; it may have many shades of colour and of earthiness, and it is particularly prone to change under the influence of slight change of health, as well as of diseases which affect the internal organs. Although the skin is clear and but slightly pigmented, there is nothing of the albino in it, for the clearest and pinkest skin may be associated with darkly tinted hair and irides.

In estimating the presence and degree of passion or want of passion, the cutaneous appendages, especially the hair, are of the first importance. Of the nails it is enough to say that in unimpassioned persons they are inclined to be thin, soft, weak, and easily bent, or cracked, or torn. They grow rather slowly and are easily cut. Deviation from the natural shape of the nails is more frequently a sign of bodily ailment than a note of character.

The cutaneous structure which calls for the closest scrutiny in detecting nerve proclivity, and therefore in reading character, is the hair-growth. We cannot measure, we cannot always infer, the thickness of the skin. We can in most cases, not by any means in all, fairly estimate the quantity of hair. The hair-growth, it is important to note, is everywhere poor, or everywhere plentiful, or everywhere intermediate between the two. In forming a judgment of the quantity of hair generally, the eyebrows, especially in women, give us, as a rule, the most valuable information. They point to many facts; they are conspicuous; they usually appear early and grow quickly. They are frequently enduring and do not change, or change but little. After early life the eyebrows grow slowly. Now and then baldness may attack the eyebrows as well as the head—in men this is perhaps the rule. Less frequently the eyebrows alone may fall off. In markedly, unequivocally, impassioned temperaments the eyebrows and the head of hair will be found to have been present, often thickly present, at birth; while another baby is for a long time bald and bare. In the same family, if one parent, no matter which, is unimpassioned and the other is impassioned, one child may be born with a head of hair and the next child may be quite hairless. It will be found, too, very commonly that the temper of thickly-haired babies is easier; they take food more comfortably, go to sleep more easily, are less afraid of darkness and of strangers; their very ailments are gone through more placidly. The observer of both children and adults should be most careful to remember that even fairly abundant *light* coloured hair may be easily overlooked and misjudged.

It has already been seen that the eyebrows commonly furnish the best test of the general growth of hair. If the eyebrows are strongly developed, so is the hair generally. It is contended here that with these characteristics of the hair-growth there runs a particular kind of nerve anatomy and physiology, and therefore a particular kind of character. If the eyebrows are abundant and the hair on the head is scanty, some ailment or pathological influence, inherited or acquired, has been at work. If the head of hair is massive, the eyebrows are usually massive also; but this rule is not so uniform. Scanty eyebrows, on the other hand, point to scanty hair generally. It is true in some, but not frequent, instances that girls and young women with spare eyebrows have a copious growth of hair on the head; but this head-growth, it will frequently be found, slowly or quickly falls off, so that before early adult age has passed away, the hair may be coiled into a wisp of only slender size. If a woman of thirty, or thirty-five, or upwards, has a head of hair which falls to the waist, it is scarcely necessary to look at her face—the existence of copious eyebrows may be very safely predicted.

The laws of hair-growth just laid down have, it is well to repeat, undoubted although infrequent exceptions. Baldness from strong hereditary tendency is much less common in women than in men, but it is occasionally met with. Baldness in women too less frequently extends to the eyebrows, but possibly it may do so. Diseases have an important bearing on the character of the hair-growth; they may attack the skin and hair directly, or they may invade them indirectly through the system generally. In these ways the head-growth, the eyebrows, and the hair generally may be seriously and even permanently thinned. Bearing these undoubted facts in mind, it must never be forgotten that it would be clearly precipitate and unjust to pronounce straight off a verdict on the character of a woman the moment her eyebrows come within the range of observation; something must be gleaned of her history, her accidents, her ailments, her inheritance, and her figure peculiarities.

In the unimpassioned woman, then, who is so because she takes after either an unimpassioned mother or father (many of the most marked examples take after the father's family), the hair-growth is universally scanty, thin, poor, short. The hairs of the eyebrows are few, small, scattered, and permit the skin to be readily seen through them. The head-hair, also, especially after the early years of life have passed away, is scanty and short. Very commonly, although by no means universally, unimpassioned women are inclined to be stout and largely framed.

With the cutaneous elements, skin, nails, hair, and fat, for fat is a structure essentially connected with the skin, there run certain striking peculiarities in the skeleton and figure. The figure, let it be noted, in its main features is determined by the conformation of the bones and the manner in which they are strung together. Certain bones play a fundamental, others only a subsidiary part. The trunk primarily controls the figure, and the spinal column controls the trunk. The impassioned person's spine throws the head well backwards as well as straightly upwards. The spine of the unimpassioned tilts the head somewhat forwards —very little it may be, or it may be very much The spine is made up of a goodly number of short bones, built one upon the other, so as to form a column of singular strength and flexibility, while at the same time it affords powerful protection to the second great nerve centre—the spinal cord. In very young children the spinal column is quite straight, but as the muscles come into action, and the upright posture is slowly gained, curves gradually make their appearance. In the perfect skeleton these curves are not strongly marked. The cervical or neck vertebra have a slight curve, the convexity of which is directed forwards. Between the shoulders, in the upper part of the trunk, the (dorsal) curve is directed backwards, its concavity giving convenient package to the heart and lungs. The convexity of the lumbar (or lower) curve is turned forwards after the fashion of the neck. If one spinal curve is slight the others are slight; if one is marked all are marked. When the curves are slight the head is planted well back upon a straight and upright neck. Easily, persistently, and without effort, the head is poised in a notably erect posture. The shoulders also are seen to be set on a strikingly backward position, so as to give a wider space from shoulder to shoulder in front, and a narrower space between the shoulder blades at the back.

In the unimpassioned male or female the spinal curves undergo certain changes. The dorsal curve, which naturally is limited to the upper part of the trunk, is found to be unusually developed and at the same time extended in length from above downwards. The dorsal curve, in fact, so involves the lower neck and the upper loin curves as to encroach considerably on the neck and loins. The dorsal curve ought to cease below at a point distinctly above the waist; but in the more passionless and active temperaments it commonly reaches the waist and not infrequently descends below it. This curve, which may be slight or extreme or between the two, alters the position of the head and neck and upper limbs in a proportionate degree. The curve and its sequences, even when slightly developed, are visible through the dress, as also are the altered position of the head and upper limbs.

The position which the skeleton naturally falls into is best seen when the given person is at ease and unconscious of observation.

An increased dorsal curve throws the head more or less forward. The neck curve also becomes more marked. If the increased curve is only slight, it gives a greater fulness to the front of the neck, which, it is said, artists look upon with a favourable eye; in severer curves the neck is conspicuously shortened, and the chin is carried more or less downwards to the chest. In the portraits of the passionless, active, and self-conscious Napoleon the chin seems to rest upon the chest.

In the thorax generally, whatever the temperament, the transverse exceeds the antero-posterior diameter. In the skeleton of the impassioned the long transverse diameter is exceedingly marked, and the chest is flat. It would seem as if the thorax were endeavouring to throw itself back and embrace the spinal column. Hence, the ribs being carried so far backwards, the spine, even at its dorsal curve, is seen to lie on an actual hollow between the two shoulders. In the unimpassioned figure, on the other hand, the antero-posterior diameter of the thorax is relatively increased;

hence its cavity from breast bone to spine is deeper; the thorax has a tendency to fall forwards away from the spine, so that at the back, on each side of the spine, it lies on a level anterior to that of the most posterior vertebral prominences. The general effect is notable. The posterior aspect of the thorax, dressed or undressed, is everywhere more or less convex; it is convex from above downwards, and what is more remarkable and more characteristic, it is convex also from side to side. In both directions the vertebral spinous projections are the most prominent objects. Hence the back in unimpassioned persons has a spherical, or round, or globular, or, in extreme cases, a pudding-like appearance. The roundness is of various degrees; it may be slight and scarcely visible, it may be very conspicuous.

It will now be easy to understand that the upper limbs, being suspended from an altered thorax, occupy an altered position. The thorax, falling forward, carries the shoulders and upper limbs forward.

The more or less round back which in so many cases bespeaks an unimpassioned nervous system, is not usually seen in children; the dorsal curve and the transverse convexity increase as years go on. Child-bearing, care, labour, and poverty aggravate them. A dorsal convexity which is only slightly visible, if at all, at seventeen will be marked at twenty-seven, especially if there has been an early marriage; it will be much more conspicuous at thirty-seven. After middle life the curve as a rule makes slower progress. Very different from this is the curve of old age, which only begins with advancing years, and is rather a falling forward of the head and neck than a positive dorsal curve.

The skeleton undoubtedly gives significant and

valuable information; but in women, more especially during the earlier years of life, the eyebrows and the hair-growth generally afford perhaps a readier criterion of nerve character than the bony framework. In men, on the other hand, it will probably be found that the skeleton, from first to last, gives a more reliable, at any rate a more easily ascertainable, index of character than the hair-growth.

Several ailments alter the shape of the bones and the conformation of the skeleton, and consequently interfere with their bearing on character. Not only do various thoracic diseases, but the tendency, inherited or acquired, to thoracic trouble produces an increased dorsal curve. Rickets, even when slight—a much commoner condition in early life than is popularly suspected—affect the skeleton and frequently give rise to increased spinal curves. Labour at all ages, especially carrying weights in the tenderer years—as when children carry babies—fosters roundness of the shoulders and back. Stooping from occupation and habit lead to similar results, especially where there is debility of the muscular and ligamentous systems. *It is difficult to give too much importance to these several influences, particularly in the less well-to-do classes.* A thin, clear skin, scantily endowed with hair-covering, associated with a perfectly and persistently upright spine, flat or concave back, and a spare figure, is a much rarer spectacle than a convex back associated with abundant eyebrows and hair.

In striving to show that certain anatomical and physiological peculiarities accompany a certain kind of nerve organisation, and denote a certain kind of character, I purposely confine myself to leading peculiarities.

In all cases, above all in doubtfully marked cases,

inheritance gives an amount of information which it is impossible to value too highly. If features, skin or complexion, hair, fat, skeleton, and figure follow one parent (and they usually follow one mainly) and that parent is of active, perhaps of busy temperament, the verdict can but rarely be an uncertain one. The child, boy or girl, which takes after an unimpassioned father or an unimpassioned mother, will be in some degree an unimpassioned person. The exceptions to this rule are rare. It does not follow that the unimpassioned character of the child is similar either in degree, or in modes of manifestation, to the unimpassioned character of the parent. It is a fanciful notion that a child may take after one parent in appearance and after the other in character. It would mean that a child has the anatomy and physiology of the skin and bones of one parent and the anatomy and physiology of the nervous system of the other. It never happens. When it *seems* to happen it will be found, seeing that all human beings have much in common, that the parents are much alike in organisation, in character, and in conspicuous features. It is not very uncommon to find parents singularly alike, and it may be very difficult to say which parent the child most resembles. But the greatest difficulty arises when the child goes back, as it not infrequently happens, to the family line of one of its parents — back to individuals unknown or forgotten.

With intermediate varieties of organisation, inheritance, and proclivity are associated intermediate varieties of character. The intermediate class of men and women form, roughly speaking, a third—probably a large third of the community. It is a diversified, interesting, and important class.

The conformation and proclivities of the unimpassioned male are (with singular unfairness) less clearly marked than in the female. Like his character they have more diversity and complexity. When a given type of body and mind in the mother is made masculine in the son much is changed, although the type remains. The laws which have been inferred from the observation of the woman's skin, and hair, and fat, and bones are it is true applicable to the man, but with important modifications. In the male the skin tends to be fresh, clear, and pink in complexion; it is far from being always so. His hair-growth is less abundant as a rule than the hair-growth of the impassioned male. Nevertheless it may *appear* to be so abundant that decisive conclusions cannot be drawn from it. The eyebrows are of comparatively little value in reading the nervous organization (the character) of the male. They may be only moderately abundant, or even rather sparing, and yet if dark and long they may *appear* copious and striking. On the other hand, unlike as a rule the eyebrows of the woman, they frequently participate in the baldness of the head, and may possibly thin in early life if the head-hair thins. So with the head of hair, although not closely packed, it may *seem* massive, and if there be no tendency to baldness it may long remain so. The face-growth is, on the whole, of more value than the eyebrows and the head-growth. Baldness very rarely attacks it. There are a few data which the careful observer may note. In the unimpassioned and active the face-growth is later in appearance; it is also often thin and scanty, or scattered, or patchy. One portion of the face-growth may be much more vigorous than another. The upper lip growth is perhaps the most constant. But all these peculiarities may be concealed with the progress of time, for the hair on the face, except the eyebrow, continues to grow for many years. The act of shaving leaves a decidedly clearer and cleaner skin and the skin continues clearer and cleaner for a longer time. Probably if it were possible to ascertain the relative number of hair-roots in a given area of the head, and eyebrows, and face, in two individuals, we should be able to say which was the more impassioned of the two. We should certainly discover that the mere appearance of the hair growth is not infrequently deceptive.

It has already been seen that in the woman the eyebrows and hair afford a readier test of nervous temperament than the skeleton. In the male, on the contrary, the skeleton will probably give more information than the hair-growths. The increased anteroposterior diameter of the thorax, the forward position of the upper limbs, the forward inclination also of the neck and the head, the general convexity of the back and shoulders—slight or marked, are as a rule clearly visible in the unimpassioned male. Such a skeleton in one who takes after an unimpassioned parent leaves little in doubt. But there must be no hasty inferences. The adventitious causes which increase the dorsal curve of the spine are probably more numerous in the male, especially of the poorer class, than in the female. Boys are less liable to the curves of muscular and ligamentous debility than girls, but they are quite as liable to the curves of rickets and pulmonary ailment, and are, perhaps, more exposed to hardship, prolonged labour, weight-carrying, and occupations which necessitate the habit of stooping. In large families among the poor both boys and girls have often to carry babies— many a deformed back is the consequence. In women the more striking peculiarities of skin and hair and skeleton lead us to observe the peculiarities of character. With men it is otherwise: we shall be led by the peculiarities of character to look more closely to the aspects presented by skin and hair and bones. If a man is constantly active and conspicuous, and still more so if he is given to be restless, or fitful, or censorious, or petulant, or discontented, or given to detraction, or anxious for notoriety, we shall naturally turn to look to his anatomy and physiology and inheritance.

Now and then the intimate associate of any given person has the opportunity of judging of two or even three generations. If the observer is a competent one, and he or she accepts the teachings of these pages, and if such teachings are true, then the organization and the character of the observed person should not be difficult to decipher or to predict.

In the impassioned female, child or adult, the anatomical characteristics are quite different from those of the unimpassioned female. Her skin is not so clear, or transparent, or pink; it is not necessarily dark or brown, but it is always more or less rich in pigment. It may be light in colour and clothed with light hair, but it is rarely a clear, bright, transparent pink. The pigmented skin is perhaps less frequently associated with prettiness, nevertheless the features are often interesting or pleasing; sometimes they are strikingly handsome. With the pigmented skin there are also found, on the other hand, features of every degree of plainness.

The more impassioned women and men also have, on the whole, a greater tendency to be lean. The rule is by no means an invariable one. And, let it be noted, that in certain individuals, both of the passionless and the passionate class, alcohol, even in small quantities, leads to the accumulation of fat, both under the skin, in the abdominal cavity, and in the structure of the internal organs.

The hair-growth in impassioned women, unless there has been some special ailment directly or indirectly affecting the skin, is everywhere abundant and striking. The eyebrows are conspicuous or even massive. The head-growth is plentiful and long; if it is even closely compressed into coil or plait, the coil or plait is not small. If it drops down loose and uncut, it falls below the shoulders, or to the waist, or even lower. As time goes on it often thins in some degree, as it does in the unimpassioned, though to a less extent; but what is left will, as a rule, fall to or below the shoulders. Time thins the eyebrows, sometimes markedly, but as a rule less than the head-hair. Hence the eyebrows, as a rule, afford the more reliable test of the vigour of the general hair-growth.

The skeleton in the more emotional temperament has notable features. The spine, save under abnormal conditions, is easily and spontaneously upright. The head is carried well erect and the shoulders are held back. The thorax is strikingly wide from side to side and inclines backwards on each side of the spine. Hence the back, even when clothed, has a singularly flat or even a somewhat concave appearance transversely between the shoulders. The concavity of the waist—nowhere a deep concavity—moreover, also extends noticeably both upwards and downwards.

To put the matter plainly: a woman who has abundant eyebrows, who tends to be thin, and who has a flat or seemingly concave back, whatever else she may or may not be, will not be a passionless woman: she certainly will not be a scold. She may be good or bad, wise or foolish, refined or coarse, amiable or ill-tempered; she will *not* be restless, fitful, petulant, censorious, and discontented.

Very few words are needed to describe the anatomy

BODILY CHARACTERISTICS OF TEMPERAMENT. 67

of the more impassioned man. In skin, and hair, and fat, and bones, the same, as a general rule, may be said of him as has already been said of the woman of similar temperament. His skin is thicker and is variously pigmented. His nails are strong and grow rapidly. He does not readily accumulate fat. His hair-growth, especially on the face, is closely packed, vigorous, and appears early. Much more than the woman, however, he is liable to baldness of the head and eyebrows. His spine is very straight, his head up, his shoulders do not fall forward, and his back is flat or slightly hollow. The ailments, and accidents, and occupations, and habits which now and then interfere with these several characteristics have been already pointed out—they are both numerous and important.

BODILY PROCLIVITIES IN THE ACTIVE AND REFLECTIVE TEMPERAMENTS.

CHAPTER VII.

LOOKING at the convex back and more or less stooping figure of passionless men and women the question naturally arises—is this condition a result of debility? Certain circumstances seem to give countenance to the view that the average health of unimpassioned persons is below that of the impassioned. Enfeebling disease frequently transforms an easy, tranquil, affectionate temperament into one of uneasiness, petulance, and lessened affections. The two ends of life are feebler than the intervening period; and in children who are not going to be active and restless, as well as in old persons who have never been so, there are often signs of a seemingly busy and restless and captious temperament. A child is fitful and wayward. An old man—and some men get into second childhood very quickly—is irritable and changeable; probably he begins to show signs of deterioration by declaring or insinuating that he is a better man than ever he was. He is "sharp" with his relatives; his mind, and policy, and temper change frequently; his changes indeed are sometimes alarming; one day he will sell his property, another day he will buy a new business, a third day he will embark on a long journey. Happy the man whose family or friends can detect senility in time and check it with a firm hand—a hand that is kind, although with apparent unkindness. In these cases it is not always easy to say how much there is of irritability, of irascibility, or of impatience ; and how much of genuine shrewishness.

But mere debility is clearly not the true explanation of the characteristics of the less impassioned temperament. The passionless frequently have good health, and the male indeed often possesses great muscular strength. A clearly impassioned person on the other hand is often the victim of weak health. It is highly improbable that a form of debility, associated with certain anatomical structures, should be transmitted with unerring certainty from parent to child, and generation after generation. Then again, the spinal curves, which are really due to debility, have definite characters, and are well known.

The more emotional women moreover are not infrequently feeble and ailing women. There is one kind of ailment to which they are probably more prone than are their less emotional sisters ; they are subject to nerve disease in its hysterical and in other forms ; they may be lame with an hysterical joint, or bed-ridden with hysterical paralysis.

The unimpassioned are not as a rule without feelings, and frequently indeed they are somewhat demonstrative or conspicuous in their affections, their dislikes, their resentments, their jealousies. But they are without deep love, deep devotion, deep sympathy, deep compassion, as they are also without deep anger and deep jealousy. But the emotions, if not deep, are often genuine, well directed, and altogether estimable. The unimpassioned are rarely so entirely devoid of passion as to avoid married life. It has been seen also that the unimpassioned female readily enters into the marriage compact. It is a curious circumstance that unimpassioned women readily become mothers, and tend to have large families. The circumstance has struck a few observers interested in physiological matters. The writer, several years ago, heard an old and experienced lecturer on medical jurisprudence declare that women of cold temperament were the more prolific. The fact is beyond question. The explanation is difficult, and can only be briefly hinted at in these pages. This much, however, may be said, that every function of life is more complicated, often indeed arrested, where nerve forces are powerful, and all the forces are most powerful in impassioned temperaments. The ascetic, the theologian, and the passionless critic of life imagine that they have settled certain difficult questions when they have called them "animal" questions. Claiming to be the friends of animals, the word "animal" still remains their expression for the bitterest contempt. We may, many of us, wish that the world of life had been other than it is—assuredly it might have been much better. This is a chapter on certain physiological aspects, rather than on the ethics, of marriage. But when such phrases as "animalism" and "indecency" are bandied to and fro, it may be replied that sexless men or sexless women who, professing to be what they are not, invade (no matter under what cloak of religious ceremony or legal enactment) the deepest privacy of others, are surely guilty of gross indecency at least, if not of cruel imposture.

One boon at any rate will follow a knowledge of the anatomy and physiology of the unimpassioned and impassioned temperaments, and of those who are neither one nor the other: the chooser in the marriage choice will choose with open eyes. One man may say here is an estimable, well-ordering woman, but life to me without ardent affection—given and received—and without warm sympathy is of little value. It is possible that another man may say—I prefer an active, industrious woman, one who is a social pattern; one who will solve for me all social difficulties; and one who will not trouble me with foolish sentiment. One woman may say here is a man of blameless character, of keen faculties, and of high attainments, a man who is active in every good work, and who is of great service to his fellow creatures, but to me life with the loftiest yet passionless philosopher or philanthropist is a burden greater than I can bear. Another woman may say, give me a husband who does not burden me with "inordinate affection," one who, it may be, will brood and sulk; but rather one who is constantly active, unresting in good works, and whose light shall be seen of all men.

Should it ever happen that, by common consent, men and women of the extremely passionless type are left out in the marriage arrangement, it is profoundly consoling to know that no one would be seriously hurt—a little injury perhaps to personal pride, probably a little social disappointment,—that would be all. For the man, at any rate, to whom domestic life is more or less of a penance, to whom social or public claims are all in all—in him no passions would be wasted, no life would be embittered.

If the theory of evolution is true, if organization and inheritance are facts, if we are human because our parents were human, if we are what we are mainly because they and their forerunners were what they were, may it not be asked if the time has not come for human intelligence and human volition to interfere in the evolutionary process? May not men say—we have been heretofore for incalculable ages the servants of evolution; the time has come for us to be partners in the process; it may yet come for us to be masters. Even if evolution is left an open question the simple truths of organization and inheritance themselves still demand that human beings should have a voice in the transmission of human nature.

NOTE ON THE PASSIONLESS AND IMPASSIONED TEMPERAMENTS IN LITERATURE AND HISTORY.

CHAPTER VIII.

If men and women may be put into large classes such as the more active and unimpassioned, the more reflective and impassioned, and the intermediate, it would be surprising if we did not discover examples in history, biography, poetry, and fiction. Unequivocal specimens do actually present themselves. Their number would be greater if historians, biographers, poets, novelists, and other observers of human nature had looked at men and women with some knowledge, or at least (and this is the chief matter) some recognition, of the significance of organisation and inheritance.

Our fathers believed that men and women were what God made them; analysis was blasphemy; and blasphemers were burnt. It would perhaps have been admitted that no possible training and surroundings could have transformed a Fuegian into a Shakspere, a Newton, or a Darwin. But here the line would have been drawn. Yet if the difference between a Fuegian and a Shakspere is one of anatomy and physiology, so also is the difference between Cæsar and Nero, between Milton and a Court fool, between Johnson and Boswell, between George Eliot and Mrs. Girling.

In Hebrew writings we are told that it is better to live on a house-top than with a brawling woman. These say nothing of brawling men. Women were not told that life on a house-top was better than life elsewhere with a brawling man. But although nothing is said of brawling men *there is no single type of character which is peculiar to one sex.* There is nothing of nerve-organization, and therefore nothing of character, which a woman may not transmit to her son, and nothing a man may not transmit to his daughter. But Hebrew opinion was invariably unjust to women: the very first woman (they believed) brought a curse on unoffending millions; women were disobedient, women tempted, women were treacherous, women brawled; women were ordered to keep themselves covered, silent, submissive; at the most they might, if deeply inquisitive, put a question to their husbands. How different the woman—ideal and real—of the old Saxon heathen: their women were true in affection, devoted in help, capable in counsel. Very curiously our own Cædmon gave to Eve a much higher character than did the Hebrew writers.

The wife of Socrates has been handed down to us as a shrew — perhaps justly so. There are good reasons however for supposing that Socrates himself was a shrew. He was always seen. He was never at rest. He gave others no rest. He questioned and lectured everybody in season and out of season. To him notoriety was life, and when tired of life he courted the crowning notoriety of an ostentatious death. Probably not a few of the martyrs were men in whom the passion for life was feebler than the ceaseless and long indulged and abnormal desire for personal notoriety. A singular incident is recorded of Socrates. One morning, in a public place, he

struck an attitude of profound contemplation as if a
new problem had just presented itself to him. This
attitude he maintained all day and all night—a whole
twenty-four hours—when he offered a prayer to the
sun-god and went his way. At noon public attention
was excited; the crowd grew, and a band of observers
remained out all night to watch him. Now no human
strength can endure for twenty-four hours one position
of abstract thought without movement, or food, or
drink. Socrates was not solving a problem; he was
seeking notoriety by conscious and more or less painful effort. The great moralist little thought when he
played his pranks more than two thousand years ago
that he was revealing to a distant generation the story
of his body, his inheritance, and his physiological proclivities. But while we must admit that excessive love
of notice is not a pleasing feature in any character,
however lofty, it is not the less true that Socrates
stands out one of the noblest of ancient figures. Who
was, and where was, his superior? Let us look back,
for a few moments, at another notable figure of another
race and of other bodily characteristics, and whose life
and passions show that he was emphatically the reverse
of shrewish—King David. When we consider the
history, genius, character, of these two we may surely
ask if the time has not come for us to hear, in school
and out of school, more of the great Greek questioner
and less of the great Hebrew psalmist.

Fable and legend bequeath to us isolated incidents
which attain significance as time goes on and knowledge grows. The legend of Lady Godiva, for example,
is a lesson in physiology. Two facts are recorded of
her—recorded by those who saw, and foresaw, no
connecting link between them: Godiva's hair was a
marvel; Godiva's compassion has become a proverb.

It was scarcely necessary to tell us of the Queen's luxuriant hair. Pity deep enough, passion deep enough to throw propriety and custom to the winds is never found under a hairless skin. We may be quite sure that Godiva's eyebrows also were abundant; that she was of spare figure; that her spine was straight, her back flat, and her head upright.

Poetry and myth came before prose and reason because the emotions develop earlier than the intellect. "Love and faith" came long before knowledge. Men may never reach knowledge, but no creature is born quite devoid of love and faith. Before men thought and questioned they sang; anatomists say, indeed, that the human larynx was once purely a singing organ—such singing as it was. Happily men do not cease to sing when they begin to think; they sing the more melodiously when brain joins in with heart.

Physiological law gave us Shakspere before Newton. As the chant of the sun-worshipper died out, the poet appeared, and portrayed the sun (sunrise, sunshine, sunset) as it appeals to the emotions—portrayed it in emotional language. Much later came the astromoner, who, while he weighed the sun, talked the severest prose. The impassioned man, however, sees poetry in the prose, and the unimpassioned man sees little but prose, no matter where he looks. To legends and to poetry the physiologist finds the key. The legends come first, long afterwards comes the physiologist.

Even in the romance and poetry of older times we recognise the two temperaments. Prince Arthur, high-souled and brave, was a passionless man; so was Sir Galahad. They were examples of a class known, or unknown, in every age. We can draw their portraits for ourselves—their scanty beards, their pink skins, and their characteristic skeletons. The sadly erring

Lancelots and the Guineveres were impassioned—passionate in all the passions. Their anatomical configuration also rises before us—called up by a wand more potent than the magician's. We can only deplore their fates and their failures, and reflect how much better the world would have fared if the Lancelots could have wedded the Guineveres, and if the Arthurs and the Galahads—partly soldiers and partly saviours—could have had their Asia or their Africa, where they might have saved or fought their fellow creatures at their own sweet wills.

In the writings of our great novelists—and these are few—few as our great historians—the passionless and the impassioned stand out with great clearness. It is perhaps easier to sketch the outer life of a people, with the capable historian, than the inner life of a hamlet, or a household, or a person with the capable novelist; for if we know our own inner selves and the inner selves of our neighbours we know the history of the world. No historian has brought his characters so closely to our vision as Nathaniel Hawthorne and George Eliot have brought theirs. We take our Arthur Dimsdales and Hester Prynnes, our Tullivers and Dodsons (all these are with us), by the hand, and tranquilly talk with them on the topics of the day. To us they reveal themselves only in part. But nature's physiologists, the Hawthornes and the Eliots, lift the veil of the routine of life, and show what lies behind it.

The scenes in the *Scarlet Letter* are full of passion—open and suppressed. Strong nerve lies uncovered and quivering before us. The spectacles indeed are too painful for frequent inspection, and those spectators who also have emotional nerve, can only contemplate them when in robust health and during exalted nerve moments. Arthur Dimsdale was rent and destroyed by conflicting passions. Hester herself, branded by those who in striving to become angels, became fiends (not an infrequent incident in history) is surely the most pathetic figure in the literature of any time or people. Nursing and needlework are feeble outlets for deep emotions; and overwhelming affection cannot be repressed by binding down luxuriant hair. In the forest scene inherent passion tore asunder the cords of convention. The woman's love was unloosened; the woman's hair fell down; the sun suddenly shone on the lovers, and the too brief transformation was complete. Who would not rejoice if there existed a providence which joined the Arthur Dimsdales to the Hester Prynnes, and handed over the Roger Chillingworths to the Dodson sisters.

Roger Chillingworth's character is not a little curious. Probably he was not drawn from life, but invented, or in some degree distorted for artistic purposes. He was passionless in the affections, but passionate in vindictiveness. If Chillingworth ever existed in the flesh he was probably an example of abnormal or degenerative change. Pathological states are probably the only explanation of certain historical and in some senses inexplicable characters: Dean Swift was one of these.

George Eliot depicts many types of our passionless and impassioned fellow creatures. One woman who was beautiful, but probably unimpassioned, did not, it is true, object to an admirer's attention; but the pretty unemotional woman rarely objects to admiration. Men cluster round her with, it may be little or it may be much, encouragement; her husband knows well that there is no danger of deeper error. The woman may be foolish and vain, but she is not wicked.

Dorothea Brooke was in every fibre unconventional

and impassioned. So also were Caleb Garth and his daughter. The *Mill on the Floss* is full of information touching body and parentage. It records the inner life of two families who supply striking examples of family organization and inheritance. The Dodsons and the Tullivers were unquestionably drawn from life. The Dodsons are passionless. The Tullivers are passionate. The Tullivers include the ungovernable, head-strong but well-meaning Mr. Tulliver (who might have been kept straight by a suitable wife as Hamlet might have been by a strong Ophelia); Mr. Tulliver's sister, the mild, patient, affectionate Mrs. Moss; and Tulliver's daughter—a true Tulliver—the high-minded impetuous, impassioned Maggie. The Dodsons are Mrs. Tulliver, her candid, irritating, and exceedingly proper sisters, and the Tulliver son, a true Dodson, taking after his mother. In an outburst of fury and exertion Mr. Tulliver is struck down with apoplexy. Bankruptcy follows and afflicts Mrs. Tulliver (a Dodson) chiefly because it disperses her tea-service and her table linen marked by a "sprig pattern;" these—china and linen—having been the consolations of a troubled life. The detestable, self-satisfied, censorious Tom never does anything wrong; the delightful, self-forgetting, impulsive Maggie never does anything right. We may, at our leisure, fill in the anatomy and physiology of the Tullivers and the Dodsons. One anatomical detail, a noteworthy detail, is filled in for us: Maggie's head of hair is a conspicuous and ever recurring feature of the narrative and, directly or indirectly, brings her much distress. To a deeply impassioned man Maggie would have been an earthly paradise; to a passionless man she would have been an uncomfortable perplexity. In one respect, at least, George Eliot towers high above all other novelists: she conceives, and depicts in her pages, the most impassioned characters, and she rouses the deepest emotions in her readers. She was herself a profoundly impassioned nature.

Charles Dickens was, by temperament, one of the active unimpassioned order. With marvellous gifts of observation and description, of wit and humour and sarcasm, he lacked deep feeling. No man of clear vision and direct expression is wholly without pathos; but it is, and Dickens's pathos was, an intellectual product. He was sometimes pathetic when he did not know it; when he wished to be pathetic and passionate he was theatrical and affected. In bodily features and proclivities, in life and habit and conduct he was as distinctly unemotional as he was pre-eminently intellectual. He was unceasingly active, given to detail, fitful and self-willed. At Gad's Hill he ran a tunnel under the highway to a plot of land on which he erected a Swiss chalet. His incessant changes there, his additions and demolitions, his constructions and reconstructions were a standing joke among his friends. When completely worn out his method of resting was to take up private theatricals and be at once stage-manager, carpenter, property-man, prompter, and chief actor. Costumes, too, and scenes—nay, even the band and the play-bills were under his direct control.

A marked feature of the unimpassioned character is seen in Thomas Carlyle—a writer who in force of thought and language has few if any rivals, and who as a provoker of thought in its noblest fields has no rival at all. But he was utterly unable to approve of the men and movements of his own time and place. Mr. Lowell pithily remarks that he went about with his Diogenes lantern "professing to seek a man, but inwardly resolved to find a monkey." In truth, it was not so much that he *would* not find a man as that, by temperament, he *could* not. He had no doubt much seeming passion—seeming anger, for example, but his anger was merely petulance on a magnificent scale. His fury was intellectual fury.

We may learn much of temperament if we closely study the lives of great men—say Shakspere, Burns, Byron and others. It has already been stated that the deeply emotional are also calm. Shakspere was known among his fellows as "the gentle Shakspere." Chaucer was called "the quiet Chaucer." Burns, with sad training and baleful surroundings, combined a vehemence and a tenderness unknown before or since.

Alas, too, how unfortunate impassioned genius has often been in domestic life. It is a physiological question. Such natures mature slowly in faculty and in judgment, in gaining and in using experience; but being impassioned and impatient—they love too early and too often foolishly. There is little doubt that the wives of Shakspere and Burns and Byron were unimpassioned women. As the wives of other men, or in other positions, those women might perhaps have done good service; being where they were they changed a few fates and much history for the worse. It has often been supposed that genius is exacting in domestic life, and demands responsive genius. Biography does not teach this; this is not true. Genius needs only peace, and affection, and sympathy—not even the sympathy born of insight, admirable as that is—the sympathy born of deep affection is enough.

It may yet come to pass that a gallery of portraits will tell us more of human nature and character than has so far been hoped for. The gallery will be more than a gallery of art; it will be a museum of body and parentage and character. But figures and unconscious poses (difficult to get) as well as faces will be needed. The figures, the heads, the hair-growth, the faces must all be absolutely faithful. It is worthy of note that the portraits of the first two women, the first two character-drawing women, of our country, one the greatest female poet, the other the greatest female novelist, disclose to us massive heads of hair and abundant eyebrows. It is the world of actual life however that we are called upon to see and read.

For the world itself is a long picture-gallery. We march from picture to picture, and at one pace. We cannot choose but march; we cannot change the pace. Not a step can be retraced, but the pictures repeat themselves in many ways. Much that is in the pictures lies outside us; much more we ourselves put into them. If we are simple they are simple; if we are complex they are complex. The pictures too are full of light and shade. Some of us heighten the lights, and some of us darken the shadows.

BODY AND PARENTAGE
IN EDUCATION, MORALS, AND PROGRESS.

CHAPTER IX.

The incidents of daily life and history are for the most part incidents in the life and action of that mysterious organisation, brain and nerve. The sun and stars are not light, and do not give light; they merely give out a force-wave, which is itself dark until it touches nerve. Thunder is silent until its silently travelling vibrations fall on nerve. So in like manner the universe itself starts into existence only when an outer mysterious something comes into contact with still more mysterious central nerve. Thus the brain makes its own world out of the raw material of circumstance—matter, force, change—which lies around it. The ocean of circumstance flows everywhere, and beats on every object—nerve alone responds, shapes, controls, creates.

It is true the universe is an enigma; but the enigma lies mainly in the inner nerve. If the brain, in mass, organisation and power were, say, six times more effective than it is, the universe would be six times less unknown; six times grander; it would have a six-fold deeper poetic significance; human conduct would be six times more finely fashioned.

The emotions, thoughts, resolves, and deeds of mystic nerve substance, when clearly seen and passionately sung, are spoken of as poetry; they are put on the stage, and we talk of them as the drama; they are discussed in Parliament and framed into laws; they seek communion with the supernatural in grove, or temple, or pagoda, or mosque, or chapel, or church, and we speak of religion; they are trained by teachers and by the world, and we discourse on education.

Everything that is known, or can be known, is part of some science, whether the science is clearly or but dimly understood. Everything that is done or can be done belongs to some art; the art may be lofty or humble, true or false, adequate or feeble. There is, moreover, no art which is not based on some knowledge—based on some, one or more, of the sciences.

The more we come to see that many arts are founded on the truths of human nature—on the truths of human nerve, the more will those arts prosper. Poets, dramatists, historians, moralists, politicians, jurists, teachers, physicians, are first of all artists in the truths of physiology. The artist will be effective or ineffective in proportion as he accepts or rejects those truths.

It is true that not all the knowledge gained by nerve can be called physiological knowledge. Nerve searches the heavens and infers certain astronomic laws; it traces the formation of the earth's crust and geological truths are brought to light. But the knowledge which tells of the direct outcome of nerve life—of sensation, emotion, thought, volition, action—this knowledge, in all its varied phases, belongs to physiology, and the arts based thereupon are nerve arts.

It is, no doubt, convenient to isolate, if in a somewhat arbitrary manner, groups of physiological facts and call them sciences. We do so when we speak of the moral and certain other sciences; but these, from a scientific, not necessarily from a practical, point of view are secondary sciences, and mere darkness and confusion follow the forgetting that the primary underlying science is physiology.

Character rests primarily on organization and its proclivities. A man is human, with human nerve and human character, because his parents were human, with human nerve and human character. His nerve and character would be other than they are had the nerve and character of his parents been other than they were.

It is inheritance then which mainly determines whether a man shall be capable or incapable, brave or cowardly, trustful or suspicious, prudent or reckless, voluble or taciturn, romantic or prosaic. Circumstance comes into play rather in detail and in smaller matters. A man is voluble because he takes after a voluble parent, but he talks more or less on the topics of the time. A woman who takes after a brave parent is brave, but her bravery probably runs to a great extent in the groove of daily life.

Even popular sentiment, which detests and rejects a "materialising" physiology, acknowledges, often unwittingly, the existence of hereditary temperaments, and talks of the "born orator," and of the poet as "being born, not made."

It is organization and parentage which primarily divide men and women into races, classes, parties, faiths. It is organization—a sad and erring organization—which, for the most part, decides who shall be criminals, or paupers, or drunkards, or libertines, or lunatics. It is organization also—a noble organization—which chiefly determines who shall be observers, thinkers, truth-seekers, truth-speakers, artists, poets. It is true the strongest stream of organization and proclivity may be disturbed by powerful side currents of circumstances; but the stream usually remains *the* stream, and side-currents remain as side-currents. Even in religion and politics nerve plays a fundamental part. Deferential nerve, submissive nerve, believing nerve, tends to one party; independent, observing, inquiring, enterprising nerve tends to another party; unreasoning, intractable, obstructive nerve tends to a third. Inheritance and organization, it is commonly but inconsistently admitted, give to races their characteristic traits. One kind of racial nerve displays enterprise, courage, persistence, restraint; another kind tends to be clamorous, helpless, help-hindering, resentful, turbulent; another is indolent, suspicious, credulous, engaging, cruel.

Thus the peculiarities of the individual, the class, the party, the faith, the race, lie hidden in nerve substance. We cannot, it is true, differentially stain these peculiarities and put them under the microscope. But physiology is still in its infancy. It once seemed impossible to measure the rate at which sensations and volitions travel on their several nerve pathways. All our marvels were once in mist-land; mist-land holds many marvels still. To pluck fresh marvels from the mist is to add not only to our common stock of knowledge but to our common fund of poetic feeling—a feeling in itself richer than the merely written rhyme.

The study of character, of education, of career, of morals, of progress, from the physiological point of view, leads us straight to first principles. And first principles, be it noted, are not buried in the quicksands of speculative philosophy where diggers have never yet discovered anything save the failures of their forerunning and their fellow diggers.

The student who searches for a key which will unlock the secrets of character may profitably reflect on Stuart Mill's experience. Mr. Mill strove long and patiently to discover the science of character. Except as a conveniently detached group of physiological truths we have seen, if we have seen aright, that no such science exists. Mill relinquished—reluctantly relinquished—his task and confessed his failure. If mere thinking could have disclosed a science, he, one of the acutest of thinkers, would not have failed. Mill fared as the traveller fares, who, seeking some treasure hidden in the east, doggedly turns his footsteps to the west. He began by putting organisation, parentage, and proclivity aside. He declared that all men begin alike.

The unconscious jokes of distinguished men are more entertaining than the conscious efforts of comic writers. Lord Chancellor Bacon believed that an old woman could blight her neighbour's pig by means of an ill-natured glance; John Wesley asserted that "Mr. Jones" had upset the Newtonian theory; Cardinal Newman affirms that incidents which, to ordinary eyes, look like cause and effect are nothing of the kind—they are a succession of actions performed by angels; Thomas Carlyle, forgetting the inherent proclivities of the French celt, believed that it was Samuel Johnson mainly who saved us from a French revolution; Mr. Froude, forgetting the proclivities of the Saxon lowlanders, declares that, had there been no Scottish Knox, England would have become a Spanish colony; Mr. Gladstone, forgetting that truth comes in late "limping on the arm of time," considers that a proposition is true which has received a wide assent for eighteen centuries—believers in witch burning held that a thing was true which had been taught up to the seventeenth—but *we* can see that they were one century short of the magical number. To cut a long story short, Stuart Mill thought that all men begin alike.

Let us look at two portraits, one the portrait of the greatest of men, handed down to us because he was great; the other a portrait handed down to us solely on the ground of high official position. All the portraits of Shakspere agree in giving him so massive a brain that half the head seems to be above the eyes. The head of a Hanoverian George was almost wholly below the orbital line.

Could any possible combination or succession of circumstances have enabled the third George to write Hamlet? Could any conceivable surroundings or antecedents have converted Shakspere into an obstinate and feeble-witted monarch? In Shakspere, and in the Georges, brain came first and circumstance a long second. The sun, the fields, the trees, the flowers, the stream, the living things, and above all human nature whispered mysteriously to every young brain in Warwickshire Stratford; only one brain was fitted (fitted by long and, to us, silent inheritance) to hear the whispers and interpret them to his fellow men.

If character is for the most part a product of organization and parentage it follows that education is mainly a physiological art. It is an art which should aim at strengthening feeble, repressing exuberant, correcting false, and straightening crooked nerve.

The first duty of the educational artist in physiology, who will come to be the one supreme, confidential "Father confessor" of the future, is to study the character, proclivities, conduct, the gifts, defects, and eccentricities of the parents. A child usually takes after one parent or one parent's family. But both sides should be studied. A child sometimes turns back to one of the father's family if it takes after the father, or to one of the mother's side if it takes after the mother; it is probably so when the offspring appears to resemble neither of the parents. A son may take after the father's side or the mother's; a daughter after the mother's side or the father's. How often we find the disappointing son of a great father to be the image of a maternal nonenity. Often, on the other hand, the son of a paternal dullard displays unexpected power—he takes after a mother of high capabilities. Edward I., a sagacious ruler, was the son of a male fool and the grandson of a male knave, hence we infer that his mother, Eleanor of Provence, had those high qualities which, in her son, changed so much in the course of English history.

Self-searchings and confessions would have for parents themselves, at a time when they greatly need it, the highest educational value. But parents must not only confess themselves, they must be judged by others also. The task of parents and teachers will not always be easy. The parents may be much alike; and frequently both will be quite average persons. Hereditary material for the trainer's guidance may not only be colourless—it may be disguised, or falsified, or misreported, or misread, or wilfully withheld. And moreover, sad to say, disease and accident are always on the watch to injure nerve and lower character. They are especially prone to step in when, in father or in mother, high nerve structures were at one time tensely and unrestingly strung.

Much training must of course be common to all young nerve. To all should be given, as far as nerve capacity and strength permit, the instruments of intellectual activity. All must be taught cleanliness, exercise, and care of body. All must be taught the hideousness of cruelty, the infamy of falsehood, and, as far as possible, the degradation of ignorance. Health, cleanliness, inquiry, truth, kindness — these are, in themselves, an entire system of physiological morality, physiological education. They are the continually thriving product of a million years. To these should be added, in due time, disciplinary and acquisitional methods. Some methods fortunately combine both training and knowledge—the study of a science, say physiology as even Mill declared, does this. There must often be a compromise between the kind and degree of discipline, the kind and amount of acquisition on the one hand, and organization, proclivity and imperious circumstance on the other. For the practical purposes of life, health, above all health of nerve, includes all the restraints; truth includes all the fidelities; kindness includes all the graces of life.

What more can be done for the individual that is not done for all, will depend on special, personal, inherited nerve. Nerve is paramount, but education can do much. It is true a young bone can be bent more easily than a young brain can be radically changed; but a young bone *can* be bent if taken in time by suitable and untiring methods. Idle nerve cannot help being idle, hence punishment is barbarous and coarsening. But idle nerve should not be lightly given up; it may come to this in the end, but it should come with kindliness and resignation rather than with despair or anger. But frequently idle nerve may be helped by patience and watchfulness. Sometimes it is merely a stage in nerve development which passes away. Sometimes it is an ailment for which the physician can do more than the formal moralist or the too eager schoolmaster. An industrious boy cannot help being industrious. Now and then, indeed, industry is excessive and is a nerve-ailment; add to this ailment an extensive curriculum, numberless examinations, an exacting and exhausting university, and the result is life-long disaster—life on a lower nerve level. One boy (or girl) has silent nerve; he should be encouraged to make little speeches. Another boy has voluble nerve; he should be taught, in some measure, to ask his questions and express his thoughts in writing. Reflecting nerve should be taught to act. Acting nerve should be taught to reflect.

The close observer of body parentage and proclivity (the physiologist) can give great help when the time comes to choose a vocation. For when nerve failings have been strengthened and nerve overflow checked, nerve proclivities have still to be reckoned with. Is it well, for example, to make a barrister of a young fellow who takes after a speechless parent? Or a science student of a garrulous youth who inherits no faculty either of observation, or reflection, or inference? Why put to a calling which demands abstract thought one who inherits a preference for detail and action? Why put to affairs the counterpart of a pensive and poetic parent?

Much young brain, too, is undoubtedly overworked. It is true that in all mental work millions of grey cells are left unused; but these cells are not independent, self-sustaining, self-acting cells. Nerve force, pure blood, oxygen, form a definite and limited sum-total. It is not thinking only that exhausts thinking nerve; the convertibility of nerve force goes much further. Powerful emotion destroys thought; deep thought destroys emotion. Excessive muscular force (notwithstanding that motor nerve-centres are more or less isolated centres) impair both thought and feeling.

What then (the question comes home to every one) is a given, individual nervous organisation capable of doing? Let us look first at nerve inheritance. If no tendency to nerve ailment is inherited, and especially if none exists on the parental side which the individual follows, if no accident has intervened in the transmission of nerve or in its training, the child may be set to work—the adult to hard work. But not otherwise. Nothing approaching to strain must be put on the brain which inherits trouble or weakness, or which has been subjected to unfavourable circumstance. The outward bodily appearance is altogether misleading. To stout limbs and red cheeks there may be joined a nervous system quite incapable of effort. While within a pale skin and delicate frame there may be a brain which close and continued labour cannot easily injure.

The wear and tear of brain or nerve is not confined to the young. To the toil (especially mental toil) of maturity are added cares which tell on nerve even more than toil. It is not easy to devise remedies. But one incalculable boon for all toilers would be the establishment of more frequent days of rest—more Sundays. One of the traditions of an indolent and superstitious time, adopted and spread (with much other superstition) by the Roman empire and the Roman sword, was the Hebrew "six days" legend with its six days' labour. Much better is the teaching of physiology: work—the life's work, thought, research, truth-seeking, science—these chiefly for three or four days; then, on the fourth or fifth day—the newer Sunday, recreation, contemplation, the solace of the arts—poetic, dramatic, musical, pictorial, and above all the surrender of self to the ennobling charms of Nature.

Meanwhile, seeing that we cannot compel the world to be tranquil, let us, as far as our individual organization permits, make *ourselves* tranquil. If "man is man and master of his fate" he can surely cut for himself a quiet pathway through a busy world.

Progress is a chapter in the history of body and parentage: a chapter which records how inner nerve and outer circumstances are both changed; how circumstance develops nerve; how nerve multiplies circumstance. Every sort of nerve is changed, intellectual, moral, and bodily. Intellectual nerve grows more acute; moral nerve more refined; bodily nerve stronger. In health the several nerve actions always keep near together. It is true that unhealthful and abnormal nerve states and actions are unhappily frequent. Intellectual nerve may be powerful and moral nerve weak; less frequently, perhaps, moral nerve is stronger than the intellectual. The disproportionate strength of body in the labouring class is the result of inheritance under long continued abnormal conditions. But even in this class it will often be found that the bodily stronger man is also the more intelligent, and the more moral. Let us, putting exceptional nerve aside, look at a few hundreds of *average* men. The hundred which have the largest sum of mental nerve and mind, will also have the largest sum of moral nerve and morals; they will, moreover, in all liklihood, have the largest sum of bodily nerve and bodily efficiency.

Nerve actions run together because nerve structures are closely related and lie side by side. Countless links join nerve-cell to nerve-cell, cell-group to cell-group, nerve-mass to nerve-mass. As a rule, the supply of nutriment is active or inactive to all alike; growth is strong, or feeble, or otherwise, in all; all go well in health; all suffer in disease. Nerve links vary in number and efficiency as do nerve cells. Mrs. Nickleby's links (and Mrs. Nicklebys are plentiful), were few: a summer's day always brought to her mind roast pig stuffed with sage and onions. Macaulay's brain was rich in links. If every copy of "Paradise Lost" or of the "Pilgrim's Progress" had been destroyed, he could have given them back to us word for word. Minds that are remarkable for memory or figures do not excel in judgment, in penetration, in imagination, in conduct; they are what they are merely because they have a certain exceptional nerve construction.

To find out the sort of circumstance which makes better nerve will one day be our first care. Some of the circumstance we can reach and change, some we cannot. Within reach is marriage, and through marriage, inheritance. Marriage is, for good or evil, the most potent nerve changer; it stands foremost in either blessing or cursing men, women, and children.* Yet physiology, which teaches all this, is the one knowledge which we, led by theologians and theologically-led poets, have ignored, jeered at, and spat upon. A few generations of, quite accidentally, fortunate marriages, in which good and helpful nerve qualities (often silent qualities) come together, and in which bad and hindering nerve is left out, give us our greatest gifts, give us our geniuses, our Shaksperes and Newtons. But, alas, the race of Shaksperes and Newtons is not kept up: less fortunate marriage, less fortunate nerve, less fortunate circumstance also, let it be added, step in and bring again the commonplace.

If a few generations can do so much for fortunate individuals, probably a number of centuries may do something for fortunate peoples. To those who preach the decadence of our race because we have no Shaksperes now, it may be pointed out that specimens often come long before the mass comes; that it took millions of years to produce *one*

---

*On marriage question, see close of chapter vii.

Shakspere, it may take at least many centuries to produce another. When the tide comes in—tide of salt water, or tide of human nerve, a long wave runs in from time to time, and shorter waves follow; Shakspere was a long wave, and in nerve waves three hundred years count for little. We have no Shakspere now, it is true, but we are all nearer to him—nearer to the Shakspere of the past, and, it may be, the Shakspere of the future in whatever shape he may come.

Great brain, great nerve, helps on progress mainly by enriching circumstance—enriching circumstance by seeing it more clearly, seeing more of it, setting it forth more truly, putting it to good use. Unhappily, now and then, great brain, like much of the smaller sort, is ill-balanced and abnormal. It is sometimes greedy, ostentatious, perhaps aggressive abroad and impoverishing at home. In private life this is a discomfort; in national life it hinders progress. Splendid warriors have often injured the peoples they *seemed* to exalt. A Cæsarless, modester Rome might still have been great. Napoleon, helped beforehand by Louis XIV., impoverished French circumstance, and thereby injured French intellect, French morals, and French body. As a rule, however, perhaps a fortunate rule, great—the greatest—brain is not overwhelming; great brain is quiet; it does not electrify; it does not domineer; it scarcely even leads. No fuss was made of the "quiet Chaucer" or the "gentle Shakspere." No one spread red cloth for Newton's feet or Darwin's.

Another field of circumstance within reach is education. We are now going through perhaps the most momentous revolution in our history; as with the actors in all revolutions we do not see it because it is so near to us. At the present moment immorality and crime is lessening so unmistakably among the young of our school districts that the ancient enemies of education are either dumb or stammer out foolish or incompatible explanation; the enemies who declared that "modern education" leads everybody astray, and the enemies who foretold unspeakable calamities in an age of "clever devils." Education, it is true, cannot all at once change hereditary nerve, abnormal, or feeble, or destructive, or dishonest nerve; but it can put an end to much brutality, coarseness, cruelty, and crime, by putting an end to the ignorance on which these mainly thrive. Eighteen years of efficient and universal schools will bear searching and significant comparison with eighteen centuries of churches.

Nerve actions, intellectual and moral, run near each other, but not quite abreast. Nay, sad to say, they are sometimes unevenly matched. Intellect leads—leads upwards in life when it sides with truths; for truths are alive, fruitful, merciful, strengthening; they are discovered, not made. Intellect leads downwards when it sides with mere opinion; for opinion confuses, enfeebles, hinders, is often cruel; it is made, not discovered.

But if intellectual nerve leads—leads well when it is good nerve, leads poorly when it is poor—it must never be forgotten that moral nerve and bodily nerve follow closely upon its heels. The moral sense constantly appeals to the intellect; the intellect cannot move without stumbling over a moral question; the body sends messages to both and receives messages in return.

Progress follows truths; it does not overtake them; it never goes beyond them. When truths were few and opinions many, when men knew little and believed much, the explanatory scheme of all things, around us and within us, was a mere list of supernatural items. If one item was given up another took its place. If, two thousand years ago, it had been shown that epilepsy was *not* due to the "possession of devils," no one would have hinted at pathological causes. Only two or three centuries ago opinion burnt women because cows died. Puritan opinion (with its good and its evil), burnt the most eagerly. Opinion would have burnt men also, if they had said that inflammation was stronger than witchcraft. Neither two thousand years ago, nor three hundred, were truths sufficiently numerous to make men compassionate; for truths, be it always known, lead men to compassion and compassion leads men to truths.

Nerve actions, we have seen, run in company. A fairly accurate, practical, and working test of progress is therefore at hand. If intellectual nerve improves moral nerve improves also; if one decays the other decays; if one utterly breaks down so does the other. If, then, we are not quite sure whether the intellect of a people, or a person, is more or is less acute than it once was, we can, at any rate, be sure whether their conduct grows better or grows worse.

A better morality then is the unfailing test of progress. And, let it be added, added on every ground and with all emphasis, that the unfailing test of a better morality is a constantly growing kindliness. Whenever and wherever there is progress every human relationship is kindlier; men are kinder to all living things; individuals are kinder to individuals; classes to classes; parties to parties; peoples to peoples. There is greater kindness on both sides (if both sides are making progress), between parents and children, masters and servants, teachers and taught, rulers and ruled. Human life is a sphere with two poles—ferocity and kindliness: supernaturalisms and opinion guide men to one pole, ascertained truths guide them to the other: the latitude and longitude of the travellers admit of fairly precise measurement.

Good brain is prone to ponder, evil brain to strike. Well-inherited, well-matured, well-circumstanced brain leans to suspense and kindliness. Poorly inherited, immature (immaturity sometimes lasts long), ill-nurtured, senile (senility sometimes comes early), degenerate, enfeebled brain leans to undue confidence, dogma, precipitancy, and cruelty.

Kindliness is stronger when it is stirred by witnessed truths than when it is based on the most eloquently spun or beautifully rhymed opinion. The sportsman, deaf to preacher and poet—perhaps himself preacher or poet—puts aside his powder and shot, when the student of physiology—the one knowledge which teaches mercy—shows him that what he took for bone and flesh, and fur, is everywhere a delicate network of keenest nerve.

It has just been said that truth is merciful and that opinion is cruel. History says this over and over again. Pagan opinion burnt Christian opinion; Christian opinion burnt Pagan opinion; Catholic opinion and protestant opinion burnt each other; Catholic and Protestant opinion joined to burn truths. Truths burn nothing. Even in our time opinion has not lost its cruel propensities. Its hands are kept off (not yet entirely kept off) opposing opinion only because truths are compassionate, have already many friends, and practically rule. Its hands are kept off truths themselves only because truths are strong and alert.

The arts console and charm the already civilized; they do little to civilize. The sciences rouse; the arts soothe. Both man and nations advance when they are roused; both stand still when they are soothed.

Rude peoples have no doubt rude arts; but arts they unquestionably have. They delight in ornament, and their daily life, so we are told, is full of ceremonial. Cannibals chant, with more or less melody, when they eat their aged and useless parents. They would probably be glad to chant and munch surrounded by great works of art, if only a choice gallery chanced to be near.

In the older and shorter-lived civilizations, which cared more for the embellishments of art than for the promptings of knowledge, brilliant orators savagely cursed their opponents, savagely (no doubt falsely) depicted them as "clotted masses" of abominable crime, savagely called down upon them every punishment which only fiends could contrive. Yet those merciless orators were unrivalled artists. Historians have often unmasked for us the artistic savage—the scientific savage, never. To this day artistically ornamented persons go forth to spill human blood animated by the strains of great musical artists.

The needful arts of government, the making of laws, the detection of crime, the administration of justice, were weak and therefore cruel arts when truths were few and held in slight esteem. If we look back at the crime and the punishment of not very remote periods we see little to choose between the ferocity of the criminals, and the ferocity of the judges.

From old times down to the moment when a few thinking, truth-loving, and therefore merciful men joined together to form our first society for the search and promulgation of "material" truths—down to that moment the bowels of the criminal were burnt before his eyes and his heart torn from his still living body. Such was the penal code of an art-led and theology-led people. For long cruel centuries men were skilled in the arts, they rhymed, and sang, and painted, and carved, and built cathedrals; for long cruel centuries men were devout, they prayed, and fasted, and wept, and worshipped; but they remained cruel: then science came and opened their eyes, and they saw themselves as they really were.

Morality also is a chapter in organization and inheritance: it is a property of that potent and poetic substance which we call nerve. It is a property not of human nerve only but of all nerve and of all that stands for nerve in the lowliest organism. Morality began when nerve began; it grew as nerve grew. The very existence of nerve was impossible without morality. The first specks of living matter had a certain moral flavour in them. If any group of living things were to lose the moral sense, and were, consequently, to offend the moral sense of surrounding life —were to rob, and ravish, and murder every living thing they came near—the moral indignation (as well as the bodily needs) of the animal world around them would quickly put an end to their existence.

It may be that animals are unconsciously moral, that they have no introspective faculty. True they formulate no moral laws; but neither did early men, neither do many men now, men too, be it noted, of deep moral instincts.

In one direction man is less moral than animals: he alone kills for mere amusement. Animals, it is true, are needlessly cruel. Daily, on every sea coast, millions of fowl slowly torture millions of fish, but they end by eating them. The ocean itself is a huge slaughter-house under water, but fish live upon fish. The cat inflicts twenty minutes of unnecessary agony on its victims; but the cat does not kill a mouse merely to carry home its tail.

In another direction, however, the morality of men rises much higher than that of animals, rises perhaps to its highest possible level. Merciful men—consciously or unconsciously merciful, kill mercifully, directly or indirectly prompted by mercy, and for merciful ends. Fifty thousand animals are selected and doomed and driven to slaughter—necessarily to slaughter if the human race is to continue to exist. The physiologist takes one of these, puts it into a deep sleep, takes from it a truth beneficent both to men and animals, beneficent alike to faithful hound and illustrious poet. It is the one fortunate animal of the fifty thousand. Out of fifty thousand deaths it would, if it had foreknowledge and choice, choose the one death allotted to it. The fifty thousand, save one, are snared, and smitten, and hunted, and shot, are speared, and fished, and gashed for coarse mastication or coarser sport.

The strangest immorality of our time is the so-called anti-vivisectionist movement: immoral chiefly because it would perpetuate the cruelty of ignorance; immoral because it prefers the falsehood of indolence to the truth of research; immoral also because, with instincts natural to the inexact multitude, it cares less for exact truth than for effect, opinion, sensation, belief; immoral because it is insincere, for while giving itself out to be philanthropic it is, at root, theological. It is theological in its motives, its methods, its objects, in its agents, its writers, its speakers, its platforms; in its dislike, not of one only, but of all the sciences. Theology at one time fought astronomy, it fought geology, it fought evolution. Each contest, however, left it a weaker force although, after each, it put on a smiling face and professed itself unhurt. And now theologians are fighting physiology, but fighting with a languor and a pallor which fittingly belong to a crusade of mediæval ghosts.

In strict truth theology has never cared for animals. Churches have disowned them. In pulpit eloquence the words of bitterest contempt are the words "four footed animal," "brute," "beast of the field." Peoples who are the most abject in their submission to theological teaching are not only the least scientific but also the cruelest peoples—witness the eye-gougers of Ireland and the bull-baiters of Spain.

One simple but searching question would bring to light much of the theological bias. If it were given out to-morrow, as a result of recent investigation, that experimental physiologists were on the eve of discovering that the first man was made suddenly; made some six thousand years ago; made out of dust; that the first woman was made from a man's rib; that both were made "perfect" and fitted to live for ever; but that shortly both fell from their perfect state--if such a prospect were confidently held out what would happen? This, unquestionably this : theologians, and "philanthropists" would demand—would justly demand, that no hindrance should be placed in the sacred path of experimental physiology.

Of the nature of morality, the question of right and wrong in daily life, little will be said here. For the purposes of conduct, of practical discussion, of teaching, we know what it is. Theologians and metaphysicians do not help us. First principles, which are for the most part physiological truths, may be said to lie in a deep, a mysterious, a dimly-lighted but not a turbid pool; the theologian plunges in professing that he, and he only, can clear up much of its mystery—but we do not see as well as we did before; the metaphysical diver follows, and every trace of clearness disappears.

Much, it is true, we do not know: but we know as much of right and wrong in the moral world as we do of what we may justly call right and wrong in the intellectual world, or of right and wrong in the bodily world. As the intellect (intellectual nerve) discerns that two and two make four, and acts, *must* act in submission to such discernment; as the body (bodily nerve) distinguishes between heat and cold and attends, *must* attend, to the distinction; so the moral sense (moral nerve) sees and knows the difference between truth and falsehood, between honour and trickery, between courage and cowardice, between kindness and cruelty, and behaves, *must* behave, in obedience to that which it sees and knows. The more or less compulsory action in each case is a first principle, a physiological truth—a truth of organization and inheritance. In each case moreover, not forgetting surrounding circumstances, action will be strong, or weak, or between the two, or abnormal *mainly* in proportion as nerve, intellectual, moral, or bodily, is strong or weak, or between the two, or abnormal.

How were men led in primitive time or in any time to believe that moral science or moral art began otherwise than other sciences and other arts? The science of grammar, for example, is merely a body of inferences, or generalizations, or laws, as they are called, drawn from the methods or facts of the speech of the best speakers. The art of grammar is nothing more than the application of these laws in our daily talk. So, in like manner, is not the science of morality a body of inferences, generalizations, or laws drawn from the conduct of the best conducted men? Is not the art of morality the practical application of these laws in our daily conduct? This human, this physiological morality has one great merit — it is capable of constant progress : a supernatural or perfect code can only remain perfect. More and more developed moral nerve, more and more enriched moral circumstance enables us to see a greater number of moral truths, to formulate purer moral laws, to do better moral deeds. The physiological is an inspiriting morality; the more it is trusted and exercised the stronger it grows.

Those who contend that moral science and moral art are beyond the reach of human effort may be invited to consider carefully what human effort has already accomplished—accomplished on this earth, in the star-space around it, in the fossil-rock within it: it may be pointed out that men have elucidated sciences as difficult as the moral science and practised arts, as difficult as the moral art.

In the primitive times of most peoples every incident which seemed inexplicable was held to have a supernatural cause. Moral incidents were not excepted; and in due time morality (moral science and moral art) was held to have a supernatural basis. If unhelped—supernaturally—unhelped water could not flow; if unhelped rain-drops could not reflect a rainbow; if the unhelped sun could not rise; if storm, and earthquake, and pestilence, and famine, and drought could not happen without supernatural interference, it was clearly inevitable that rude peoples should everywhere see a supernatural finger in the simplest moral sentiments—"do not kill;" "do not steal;" "do as you would be done by." This much was inevitable, no matter what the time, or country, or race, or religion, or what the popular conceptions and popular "revelations" of an imaginary supernaturalism.

It was inevitable, too, when it was believed that moral precepts had a supernatural origin, that religions (schemes of man's relationship to the supernatural) should be fitted on to them. Moral teachings were feeble, and made little progress until the spirit of inquiry sapped the belief in their supernatural basis—then they moved, and move now, with continually increasing speed. Religion was constrained to follow. When morals were coarse religion put on thumbscrews; when morals improved, better men, kindlier men, infused something of kindliness into their religion. At one time the theological scheme held that a slave was "his master's money," that wine "cheered God and man," that the sick were to be healed by prayer and anointing with oil, that women were to be kept silent and covered. Now, after much "reconception" and "reconstruction," by men who, thanks to human civilisation, were better than their scheme, it teaches quite the reverse; slavery is an abomination, wine is accursed, the sick are taken to scientific experts and hospitals; women are called to the easel, the desk, the laboratory, and the platform; in short, at the present pace of omission, as well as of the reconception and reconstruction of supernaturalism, there will soon be nothing left to reconceive and reconstruct. It is a human and ever-growing morality—a human and ever-growing knowledge—which bring civilisation. The greatest achievement of civilisation is that it has done something to civilise religion.

But the unawakened multitude—happily a diminishing multitude — affirm that if belief in supernatural rewards and punishments were to cease, morality would cease also. Let us see: it is of all matters the most momentous. Passing over the significant circumstance that supernatural awards can have but little effect when believers themselves are ashamed of hell and desire to put off heaven to the latest moment, there remains the unanswerable argument that, while supernatural beliefs are growing feebler and supernatural ideals paler, morality itself—morality in all its aspects, is growing stronger day by day. In every direction physiological morality has gone beyond the theological.

In strict truth theological moralists deceive themselves: they and their theology participate in the very progress which they have done so much to hinder, but which, they *now* declare, is *their* progress—a progress which they have always helped and loved. It is so with all decaying supernatural systems. A dying supernaturalism may be likened to a lay figure which each generation clothes with its own civilisation. The latest generation decks out the ancient figure with its newest robes and then exclaims it lives! it lives! "Cavillers are bad-hearted men; their cavil is as old as the hills, and has been brought to shame a hundred times." It was so with the decaying supernaturalisms of ancient Greece. It was so in Rome. It is so with us.

It would, indeed, fare badly with morals if they had no other than a supernatural basis. If men were not subject to physiological penalties; if their conduct in its moral aspects could be hidden from their fellow men; if they had no inherited or nerve morality; if, in short, conduct were founded on a supernatural basis only, and were visible only to a supernatural eye, then morality at least, whatever else might remain, would vanish from this earth.

In theological speech by a curious but, perhaps, not undesigned and not inexplicable insinuation, morality has practically come to be synonymous with chastity. Theft, murder, cruelty, are mere trifles which may be left to a flesh-and-blood policeman; but chastity calls for superhuman care. Chastity or the entirely faithful union of one man to one woman and of one woman to one man, will always be the one priceless, the one most ardently longed for of human treasures. But human physiology, human nerve, human morality, human love, human faith, human truth, human honour—not to speak of human jealousy—will take good care—will take the best care of chastity. Human forces, though constantly growing in success, do not, unhappily, always succeed. Superhuman forces, however, fare no better; no better in history, sacred or profane, Jewish or Gentile; no better in daily life.

It may be that chastity will not always conform itself to the clerical formulæ of the sixth, or eighth, or any other century. It may be that the teachers of the legends, the characters, the polygamies, the concubinages, the short and easy divorces, the virgin captures, the ordeals, the witchcrafts, the devil-possessions, the rapacities, the slaveries, the wholesale slaughters of supernatural belief will not much longer be looked to as the fittest guides either to sexual purity or to morality in general. Lofty characters from Milton to Mill have protested against their teaching. Wise and courageous men and women, not less moral than their fellows, have put protest into practice.

In matters of sexual morality, as in all other matters, the older moral nerve could only devise supernaturalisms. The newer human moral nerve learns and teaches; it observes, and reflects, and reasons, and infers, and marvels; it restrains here, it releases there, it lifts up everywhere.

If, on purely human grounds, and in positive disobedience to supernatural commands, a man refuses to burn his neighbour's wrinkled grandmother for a witch, he will, also on purely human grounds, refrain from dishonouring his neighbour's comely daughter.

The greater truths are the later they appear. Later seekers, too, have a clearer vision, a stronger hatred of complacent ignorance, and a deeper compassion for human needs. Still again, why is nerve inquiry latest? The answer is surely clear. All history gives it. Primitive atmospheres, mental and moral, were thickly peopled with supernaturalisms, much, in fine, as still more primitive mud was crowded with now extinct monsters. *Supernaturalisms filled and blocked all avenues to knowledge;* they choked truth-seekers on every threshold. Perhaps all this was inevitable; for the evolutionary exigencies which slowly called forth and then slowly forsook the mammoths, created also the supernaturalisms, which now are left to slowly die.

Ages of progress, beginning with savages and ending with students, are like ages in geology—they have each their dominant and special features; but mixed with these are traces of a past and signs of a coming time. If we glance down the line of human eras and look narrowly at savages and sorcerers, at ghosts and gods and devils, at prophets and priests and miracle-workers, at saints and schoolmen and theologians, we shall nowhere see either the wish (morality was not ripe for this) or the power to distinguish between phantasms and facts; nowhere a thought about the age and formation of this or other worlds; no thought of the non-creatability and non-destructibility of matter or force; none of the continuity of phenomena; none of the evolution of living forms by sparing survival with vast destruction; and, assuredly, nowhere one straw's care for the structure and use of grey cells in brain matter.

Evolution is the way, diverging for a moment, which nature (the assemblage of all truths) has of repenting the past; and nature is now taking the control of her affairs from the priesthoods of supernaturalism, and is putting them into the hands of the nobler moralists, who seek, and sift, and reverence truths.

Brain or nerve is man. All else, that is human, is merely convenient appendage. There are, indeed, *two* physiologies—one of the brain, which is primary and culminating, and another of the appended body, which is altogether subordinate. What the brain is, so will the outcome of life be. A dog's brain is fitted for dog-intellect, dog-morals, dog-feeling, dog-action; human brain is fitted for human intellect, human morality, human feeling, human action. So far as the sum of a man's life is superior to the sum of a dog's life, precisely so far is a man's brain superior to a dog's.

In organisation and construction, in composition, in development, in nurture, in its sheltering mechanism, and, above all, in its action, brain is at the summit of known things. It rises as much above all other matter as mind rises above every other force. Brain stands alone. Slowly, through inconceivable periods, it grew in weight, in delicacy of structure, in range and potency of function, in hereditary wealth. Meanwhile blood slowly ripened for its support; bones slowly stiffened, and grew, and lifted it up; muscles slowly gathered together and attuned themselves to its commands.

"But this interpretation of nerve and life is gross, mechanical, materialistic." If it is true, we must, alas, submit to be gross, mechanical, materialistic. "Nay, such teaching will inevitably lead us to perdition." If it be true we have no alternative; we must, with whatever courage we can muster, go to perdition.

If such "views are true—inexorably, cruelly true—

they are nevertheless cold and mean." Ignorance has always called kowledge cold. Alchemy said that chemistry was cold. Astrology declared that astronomy was cold. Gravitation was cold. The development of an eye from a sensitive bit of skin during inconceivable eras was a very cold proceeding. Ghosts, and witches, and spirits call light, and heat—nay the very sun itself, cold.

Many words are despots at some period in their lives. "Materialism" and "supernaturalism" are two of these. The word "materialism" still unmans, and the multitude is still timorous—timorous by reason of inheritance, of long training, of early menace, and fair-seeming promise, and impressive adjunct. A mere word will blanch the timid cheek if inheritance and circumstance have already blanched the timid brain. When we have discovered what matter is, have measured its potencies, mapped out its limits, penetrated its mysteries, exhausted its poetries, thought its highest thought, felt its deepest feeling, when we have moreover shown up its shame and laid bare its terrors, it will be time to be ashamed and afraid of matter. In strict reality, however, the student of truth does not know enough of matter to call himself a materialist; he is simply a *non-supernaturalist.* Supernaturalisms arose in the babyhood of peoples, and survive only because they are instilled into the babyhood of individuals.

The future too, no matter how scientific it may be, will assuredly have its poets—those who will make truth more passionately and more musically true. And fuller knowledge being revealed to them, they will be juster in thought, deeper in feeling, loftier in purpose. The mountain peak will not move them the less because they will be able to trace it back, through unknown time, to minute life underneath the ocean.

A Danish forest will not the less confide to them its solemn secrets because they see, buried under it, fossil forests and, deeper still, the handiwork of early men. For them human nature will not be the less exalted because they discover that thought and feeling are born in mysterious nerve homes, and travel too and fro along strange nerve pathways. The poetry of the present will not come home to them the less because they can also decipher the volumes of extinct poetries.

One thing at least grows clearer and clearer: the onward movement of mankind will neither be checked, nor jostled out of its groove, nor turned at an angle. Our race, in its progress, may be said to be cutting its way through a dense forest. Many voices are heard in the gloom. The theologian—say Cardinal Newman, with clear and majestic voice calls upon us to return to the old paths: that cannot be. The "inspired" writer—say Thomas Carlyle, with startling gesture and vehement speech, bids us be stirring; he does not tell us how to stir or whither. The student of science —say Charles Darwin, puts a lamp to our feet, shows us where we are, how we came, and how, all helping and all needing help, we may best go on our way.

[FOR INDEX SEE FULL TABLE OF CONTENTS.]

www.ingramcontent.com/pod-product-compliance
Lightning Source LLC
Chambersburg PA
CBHW020131170426
43199CB00010B/719